Bad Blood

The Violent Lives of John Wesley Hardin, His Brothers, and Associates

By *Norman Wayne Brown* & *Chuck Parsons*

EAKIN PRESS 🎭 Fort Worth, Texas
www.EakinPress.com

Acknowledgments

We are thankful to Ron Chrisman at the University of North Texas Press, Denton, Mark Boardman, editor of *The Tombstone Epitaph*, and Roy Young of *Wild West History Association Journal* for giving permission to republish some of the stories in this anthology of the Hardin brothers and some associates. A special thanks to Dianne Webb, who provided information and *Bible* records on her ancestor Charles M. Webb. To the late Jeff D. Hardin, grandson of Jeff and Mary Taylor Hardin.

Thanks to Charlotte Pool who provided the photograph of Jeremiah Alexander Ferguson, Marc Coker, the late Jack Caffall, Tobin Armstrong, Kurt House, and Donaly E. Brice. Also, to Bob Boze Bell of *True West* magazine and Dr. Ken Howell, Executive Director of the *Journal of Central Texas Studies*. To Linda Rudd for providing a breatthrough on the depth of "Gip" Hardin. To those we may have overlooked, our apologies.

Group photo on cover: Standing from left: Mannen Kimbro, Jim Denson, Ferdinand Brown, James Monroe "Doc" Bockius, Seated from left: Jim Clements, Joseph Hardin "Joe" Clements, Mannen Clements. Image made in Abilene, Kansas 1871. *Chuck Parson Collection.*

Dedication

In memory of Jeff D. Hardin, grandson of gunman Jefferson Davis Hardin. Also, in memory of Jane Bowen Hardin, who other than the joys of her three children, sorrows greatly brought her down in spite of her love for John Wesley Hardin.

Table of Contents

Chapter One
John Wesley Hardin's Birthplace

By Norman Wayne Brown

This story was published by *True West* in March 2017 issue, titled *The Birth of a Wicked Son Reimagined*. *Reprinted with permission.*

Notorious gunfighter John Wesley Hardin was in the midst of writing about the bloody career surrounding his life story when lawman John Selman killed him at the Acme Saloon in El Paso, Texas, on the night of August 19, 1895. John's children inherited his estate, which included his autobiography. It was published in book form and titled *The Life of John Wesley Hardin, as written by himself.* He misrepresented himself many times throughout the book, starting with his opening statement, which read: "I was born in Bonham, Fannin County, Texas, on the 26th of May, 1853."

One historian made a bold attempt at questioning his birth year based solely on Federal Census records. Most historians know

John Wesley Hardin in Abilene, Kansas, 1871, at the end of a cattle drive. *Courtesy Robert McCubbin Collection.*

Reverend James G. Hardin in later life according to Fannin County historian Ronnie Atnip.

Earlest known photo of Reverend James G. Hardin. *Courtesy Robert McCubbin collection.*

that census records are often filled with erroneous information. John Wesley Hardin's birth date remains as he claimed. But the deadly gunman was not born in Bonham. A researcher, Ronnie Atnip, set forth to figure out the true birthplace, beyond the grave.

John's father was James Gibson Hardin, a circuit-riding Methodist preacher, family man and American Indian fighter. He was born on March 2, 1823, and grew up in Wayne County, Tennessee. He married Elizabeth Dixon in Navarro County, Texas, in 1847. They moved to Fannin County, where their first son, Joseph, was born in 1850. The Rev. Hardin died, at the age of fifty-three, in August 1876 and was buried in an unknown grave somewhere in Red River County. He wrote a letter to his daughter-in-law Arabella Hardin shortly before his death, providing detailed directions to his farm in Red River County and while not proven, it is logical to believe that he was buried in a private plot on his farm.

When Dr. Richard C. Marohn's biography *The Last Gunfighter: John Wesley Hardin* was published in 1995, the 100th an-

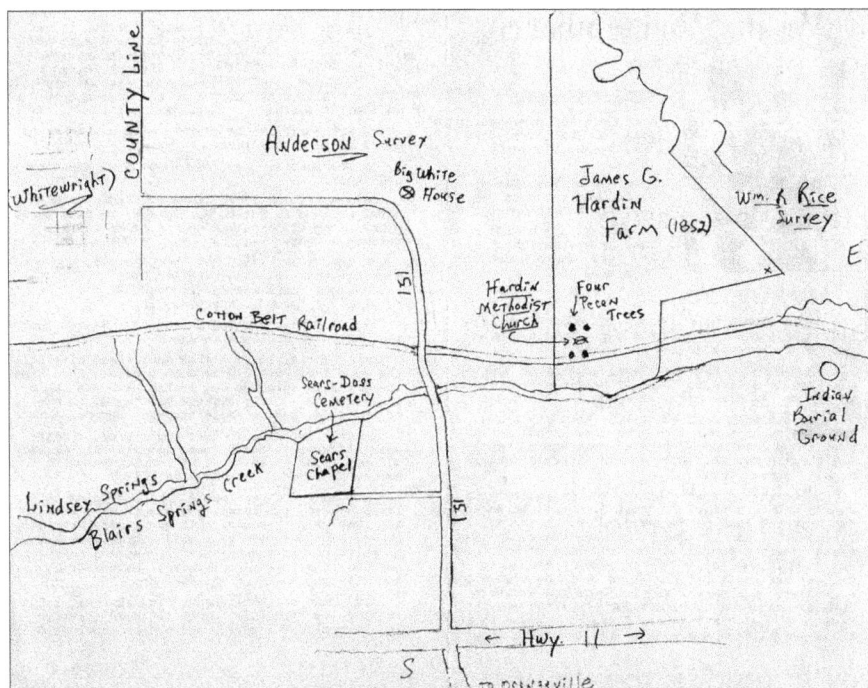

This map shows the exact spot where Reverend James G. Hardin's land was located. Within the square of Pecan trees was an early day Methodist church which also served as a school and living quarters for the Hardin family. *Courtesy Ronnie Atnip.*

niversary year of Hardin's death, readers learned: "apparently, Hardin was born near Blair Springs on Bois d' Arc Creek, near Orangeville." The biographer derived that information from a communication by Cleburne Hardin dated February 7, 1984. Cleburne was the son of Jefferson Davis and Mary Taylor Hardin; Jeff was John's younger brother. Yet the location of the farm has been elusive for years.[1]

Ronnie Atnip, a real estate agent and Fannin County Historical Commission president, diligently searched for the site. One day in 1995, Atnip met Tom Scott, who had been given a copy of an old deed indicating James G. Hardin, John's father, had bought a farm in Fannin County; the deed also referenced a church. Atnip knew Fannin County well, as he had located land many times for prospective buyers. Being a historian and Western history fan, he took it as a challenge to try and pinpoint the Hardin farm. He also wondered if that was John's birthplace. Scott told Atnip that the land was out of the Lindsey Survey and was located somewhere east of Randolph. That turned out to be the wrong area. Research revealed that the Rev. Hardin purchased 129 acres on August 7, 1852, just nine months prior to John's birth. A little over two miles east of present-day Whitewright, ten or more miles west of Bonham, the land was part of the William Rice Survey. A man named Anderson hired William F. Lindsey to conduct the survey. This resulted in the deed being misfiled as the Lindsey Survey at the county courthouse.

Adding to the

John Wesley Hardin's younger brother Jeff D. Hardin and wife Mary with sons Cleve [Cleburne] and Joe. It was Cleburne who told author Dr. Richard Marohn that his brother John Wesley was born on Bois d'Arc creek in Fannin County. The statement has proven to be accurate.

confusion, the deed renamed Blair Springs Creek as Lindsey Springs Creek. The Rev. Hardin built a Methodist church on the southwest corner of his farm near Blair Springs Creek, not Bois d' Arc Creek, as Cleburne had told Marohn. Bois d' Arc runs on the north side of the property. The church, which also functioned as a school and the Hardin home, was built out of logs and located in the middle of four large pecan trees. Atnip found the huge 143-year-old pecan trees in 1995, located just where they had been in 1852. They can easily be seen from Farm to Market Road 151, just east of Whitewright. The Rev. Hardin took a year off from his circuit riding until son John was born. The family moved shortly afterwards; John may have been told he was born near Bonham since Whitewright did not exist until years after his birth. The Orangeville referenced by Cleburne was the closest settlement during the 1850s.

Atnip made two aerial views to pinpoint the farm. As a Fannin County historian, he knew that the spot he pinpointed as the Rev. Hardin's farm was a historic camp site for Indians, travelers, buffalo hunters and Texas Rangers. It was also the spot where famed Alamo defender David Crockett camped and traded the long rifle, he brought from Tennessee for one with a shorter barrel before riding out to the area known today as Ozona. He left his "Old Betsy" long rifle with his son in Tennessee and that rifle was eventually donated to the Alamo Museum. It is unclear exactly what rifle Crockett traded for near the Hardin farm. Also, without a name, it would be difficult to substrate the story of a rifle trade.

"Years later, the owner of the long rifle allegedly donated it to the Alamo museum and that rifle was claimed to be on display. Regardless, the rifle Crockett used at the battle of the Alamo would have been confiscated or destroyed by the Mexican army. The man who is said to have donated Crockett's rifle lived in

Ronnie Atnip is holding a limestone block that was a foundation support of the Hardin combination home, church, and school. An interview with an early pioneer informed Atnip that he recalled seeing the limestone block as a kid wading in the nearby creek. He said those blocks were also used as steps.

Cast iron artifacts found at the Hardin homesite by Mr. Atnip believed to be the remains of a stove or other early day household items.

Whitewright," Atnip reported.

Atnip personalized his search for Hardin's birthplace by reading the entries of a scrapbook owned by the Rev. John W. Connelly, a captain of combat troops during the Civil War. After the war, he spent years teaching and preaching to the Choctaws in Indian Territory and was nicknamed "Old Choc." In the scrapbook, Connelly noted how James G. Hardin became one of the early-day Methodist preachers to be heard in the state of Texas. The state's oldest Methodist church, organized in 1833, is McMahan's Chapel, a few miles east of San Augustine.

Ronnie Atnip is credited with finding Hardin's land and he is standing by one of the old Pecan trees mentioned in the deed. In 1995, all four Pecan trees were still standing after a century and half.

Connelly didn't shy from his opinions. He pointed out that the Rev. Hardin was "lukewarm" when preaching of fire and brimstone. He added: "Reverend Hardin's wife Elizabeth was a most elegant Christian woman. They furnish an illustration of the fact that very pious parents sometimes raise very wicked sons." His most monumental statement: "the first Methodist preacher I ever heard in the state was Rev. Hardin, father of the notorious John Wesley Hardin. He was living in that old schoolhouse at the time and in it John Wesley Hardin first opened his eyes upon this world."[2]

Atnip's discovery that the notorious gunfighter's birthplace was actually a settlement that came to be called Whitewright hit the headlines of the Bonham newspaper and word spread. During the research phase of *A Lawless Breed*, a fresh biography on Hardin written by me and Chuck Parsons, Chuck made a field trip to the Hardin home site and nearby cemetery. The property is adjacent to a registered Longhorn cattle ranch.

John Wesley Hardin, being a pioneer cattle trail driver on the Chisholm Trail to Abilene, Kansas, would be proud knowing Longhorn cattle are grazing peacefully around his first home, even though he will mainly be remembered, not for his cowboy career, but as one of the most deadly of early Western gunfighters.

When Ronnie Atnip returned on another field trip to John Wesley Hardin's early home, he was drawn to the Sears-Doss Cemetery located near the Hardin farm. To his surprise, Atnip made a great grave discovery. While searching the burial grounds, he found the headstone for Billy Dixon's grave. Billy was killed as a teenager in 1868 during the post-Civil War Lee-Peacock feud. Hardin historians believed Billy was buried in another area of Texas . . . until Atnip solved the mystery.[3]

When *True West* ran the article on Hardin's birthplace, this statement was made, " Billy and brother Simp were said to be John Wesley Hardin's cousins, according to the gunfighter's autobiography. The proof was not found at

After locating Reverend Hardin's land, Mr. Atnip ventured out and visited the nearby Sears-Doss cemetery and discovered the grave of Billy Dixon, mentioned by John Wesley Hardin in his autobiography as a cousin who was killed in the Lee-Peacock feud. The location of Billy Dixon's grave has been a mystery for historians for many years. When author Chuck Parsons heard about Atnip's find he visited and was taken to the cemetery to see the headstone.

the time. Since that article was published, it was discovered that John Wesley Hardin's mother, Mary Elizabeth Dixon Hardin was a daughter of a second-generation Irishman named William A. Dixon. John Hugh "Irish Jack" Dixon was a third generation Irishman, and his sister was none other than Mary Elizabeth Hardin. Therefore, John Wesley Hardin and Simp and Billy Dixon were first cousins. Although beyond proving today, Hardin is suspected to be among the men who killed Billy's murderer, Unionist Lewis Peacock."

However, there were those two great discoveries about John Wesley Hardin's true birthplace and the locating of Billy Dixon's grave.

Chapter Two

The Killing That Put Hardin on the Run

By Norman Wayne Brown

This story was published in *True West,* November 2016 issue. Please note new information has been discovered that will update and/or change some of the information in this story and in other chapters. *Reprinted with permission.*

Just who was Charles M. Webb? Charlie M. Webb's claim to fame came when his plan to kill notorious gunfighter John Wesley Hardin backfired. (It may not have been planned.)

Webb first appeared on the Texas scene in Brown County, where he was selected as a lieutenant in the Texas Rangers, serving under Captain James "Jim" Connell. Activated in January 1874, the company disbanded at the end of March, due to lack of state funds. Webb was then hired as a deputy sheriff of Brown County.

One theory: When Webb learned that Hardin had a price on his head, dead or alive, he must have decided to go bounty hunting. What other business could he have had to ride outside his county to the town of Comanche? On May 26, he found out Hardin and his cousins were in the saloon, celebrating Hardin's 21st birthday and his win at the horse races that day.

Once Webb determined which man was Hardin, he introduced himself. Immediately after, Hardin claimed that Webb drew his pistol and fired at him; the bullet grazed him on his left side. The Dixon cousins and Jim Taylor fired their pistols at Webb, who fell to the ground dead. Years later, Hardin wrote a letter to his daughter claiming that he had killed Webb in self-defense. Jim Taylor claimed he was the one who killed Webb.

Another theory was Webb may have been lured to Comanche by the Hardin faction, in retaliation for the arrest and killing of some of their gang. A number of articles have been written in relation to his being in Comanche and the fatal gunfight.

The killing of Deputy Webb put a millstone around Hardin's neck and led to the lynching of his older brother, Joseph, and his cousins Tom and Bud Dixon. Hardin sent a cousin, J. D. Hardin, to Kansas to sell his cattle herd so the outlaw could use that money to escape capture. Some historians believed John Wesley sent his little brother Jeff D. Hardin to Kansas. That was not the case. His brother Jeff D. was only age thirteen at the time and riding up the trail by horseback to Kansas through Indian Territory would have been a near impossible feat. It was John Dixon Hardin, his first cousin who rode to Kansas and disposed of the herd. His trip was apparently uneventful and upon his return, gave the money to John Wesley.

Hardin evaded the law until his arrest three years later, on August 23, 1877, in Pensacola, Florida. Hardin did not speak in his own defense at his trial, and testimony claimed he had insulted Webb, who just happened to be in Comanche. Hardin was sentenced to twenty-five years at Huntsville's state prison in Texas. He was pardoned after sixteen years and went on to work as an attorney. Hardin paid a high price for what may or may not have been self-defense.

Up until now, Webb's past has been a mystery. Texas alone has internment records of 111 Charles Webb's and ten Charles M. Webb's. None have

Charles M. Webb's headstone. A Texas Ranger cross was added as well as a small Civil War Marker. Daughters of the Confederacy decided he was Charley Webb who served under Quantrill. This Webb did not serve in the military. The marker represents false information. *Norman Wayne Brown collection.*

birthdays that are even close to that of our Webb. Some historians have suspected Webb of fighting with Quantrill's raiders during the Civil War. The name Charley Webb appears on a muster roll, but our Webb, born on May 2, 1848, would have been too young to officially serve in the war.

Yet Kentucky may (does) hold the key. In the northern part, in Cynthiana, is Indian Creek Cemetery, with graves for the Reverend Charles Webb and his wife, Elizabeth. could these Webb's be related to our Charles M. Webb?

The 1850 census for seventy-eight-year-old Charles and sixty-eight-year-old Elizabeth shows their household included daughter-in-law (actually she was a daughter) Huldah Webb, age thirty, and her son, (nephew)

John Dixon Hardin headstone. He went by J. D. and was a first cousin to John Wesley Hardin. He was the J D. Hardin who went to Kansas and sold Wes Hardin's cattle. *Norman Wayne Brown collection.*

Charles M. Webb, listed as age one. Charles is without a father in this home, but his father was likely (was not) William Webb, buried in Indian Creek Cemetery in 1848, the same year of Charlie's birth.[1]

By 1860, Huldah is deceased or remarried, as no record could be uncovered for her. Charles is listed on the census as age twelve and living with his uncle (not his uncle) Hamlet L.

Webb and aunt (stepmother) Nancy, in Harrison County. He owned property valued at $2,200, land probably in error. In 1870, Charles is twenty-two and working on a farm. That's the last record for Charles in Kentucky or any other place until he shows up in Texas's Brown County.

In the year 2020, a fresh article was published titled *Deputy Sheriff Charles Webb's Last Gunfight, The Tombstone Epitaph*. Contact was made with a descendent who has bible records. Huldah was an aunt and not his mother. His uncle Hamlet was actually his father. A later chapter covers the latest research findings on deputy Webb.

This Kentucky traveler, the grandson of a preacher, just may have been killed by the son of a preacher. Hardin's preacher father had named his son after John Wesley, the founder of the Methodist denomination of the Christian church.

Hardin lived by the gun, and he also died by the gun. A little over a year after the killer was released from prison, on August 19, 1895, Constable John Selman fired several fatal shots at Hardin in the Acme Saloon in El Paso, Texas. Selman also claimed self-defense for the killing, but he did not end up in prison. He was shot dead by U.S. Marshal George Scarborough in 1896 while awaiting a retrial.

Chapter Three
John Wesley Hardin's Behavioral Disorder

By Norman Wayne Brown

This story was published by *The Tombstone Epitaph* in July 2019 issue. The title was *Drunk and Disorderly, A look at the psychology of Gunfighter John Wesley Hardin*. *Reprinted with permission.*

When the latest biography was written on Texas notorious gunfighter John Wesley Hardin, by Chuck Parsons and this author, we did not dwell on his behavioral disorder.[1] Another author, Richard C. Marohn, did diagnose Hardin with a disorder in his biography, *The Last Gunfighter*.

Accordingly, he pegged Hardin with a narcissistic behavior disorder, which goes beyond anti-social behavior. Narcissists are great manipulators. They can spot the needs, emotions, and weaknesses in those around them and use that information to their advantage very quickly with no sense of regret. They do not have a conscience in this sense because they do not hold themselves responsible for the consequences of their actions; they simply work with the information available. This behavior fits John Wesley Hardin to a tee.

John Wesley Hardin claimed in his memoirs that he was born in Bonham, Fannin County, Texas, on the 26th of May 1853. He was correct about the county but was born on a farm just a few miles southeast of Whitewright. When deputy sheriff Charles S. Webb was killed by the Hardin faction in 1874, Hardin later fled the country and started visiting Pensacola, Florida, to drink and gamble. He was arrested by Texas Ranger Lt. John Armstrong and local law enforcement aboard a railcar at the Pensacola train depot in August 1877. Armstrong returned Hardin to Texas, and he was sent to Huntsville prison to serve twenty-five years for the killing of Webb. Hardin had been avoiding apprehension for approximately three years and three months.

After Hardin's pardon from Huntsville prison in 1894, he soon settled in El Paso, Texas, where he practiced law and was half owner of the Wigwam saloon. Being he was killed on the night of August 19, 1895, in El Paso, no head doctor in modern times could invite him to their couch and get him to talk about his misgivings or poor potty training. What Marohn based his diagnoses on was documented evidence of Hardin's actions from adolescent years through his adult life. He also relied heavily on the letters written by Hardin to his wife Jane while he was incarcerated. He also took into consideration the parents of Hardin and how he was raised. Apparently, what Marohn did not have was a letter written by a childhood friend who claimed to know John Wesley Hardin better than anyone on earth, except his parents and siblings, of course. Perhaps the letter could support the Marohn diagnosis.[2]

There were two attorneys who wrote about John Wesley Hardin. One attorney feared him and the other adored him. First was J. W. Thomas, who wrote an article appearing in *The Taylor County News*, Abilene, Texas, on August 30, 1895. J. W. Thomas was district attorney for Comanche and other counties in his district back in 1871. He had developed a great fear of John Wesley Hardin and had been introduced to him at his father Reverend James G. Hardin's home in April or May of 1873. Until then, he knew John by reputation only.

Thomas had heard John's brother Joe say, "John has killed thirty-eight men and I think you [Thomas] will be number thirty-nine."

John had been in Thomas's office a number of times with brother Joe. Thomas never told anyone about knowing or seeing John due to fear for his life. When John Wesley Hardin visited his office Thomas said, "John was pleasant in conversation and had considerable culture, but there was an indescribable feature about him. His eyes were very large and set well back in his head and he appeared to look in every direction at once, and in every motion, he was as quick as a hummingbird.

Years later, on November 2, 1931, attorney W. B. Teagarden[3] of San Antonio, Texas, penned a letter to Mrs. Charles Billings of Nopal, Texas. Mrs. Billings was Mollie Hardin, daughter of John Wesley Hardin. Mollie married Charles R. Billings in De-Witt County, Texas, on December 16, 1894. Nopal is a near ghost town in DeWitt County, so Mollie and Charles never ventured out to find greener pastures.

Teagarden started his letter to Mollie by stating he had read in the newspaper about the death of her father, John Wesley Hardin and her sister Mrs. Lyons. Mrs. Lyons was Jennie Hardin who married John Lyons in Karnes County, Texas, on October 9, 1898. For years Mr. Teagarden was unable to obtain an address for Mollie or John Wesley before he was killed in El Paso. Teagarden's motive in his letter was to provide Mollie with a positive character assessment of her father, who was not only his childhood to adulthood friend, but also his protector. That probably made Teagarden's assessment somewhat, if not completely, biased.

W. B. Teagarden wrote to Mollie that he was an attorney and a neighbor and good friend of Texas Governor James Stephen "Big Jim" Hogg, which led to bending the governor's ear and gaining his friend, John Wesley Hardin, a pardon from the Texas state prison at Huntsville. He said, "Hardin was convicted for the killing of deputy sheriff Charlie Webb of Brown County, Texas. Bud Dickson [Dixon] killed Webb and not Hardin. However, the witnesses could not identify anyone, and the district court did not allow Hardin to take the stand. He was convicted based on his reputation."

What were the traits that led Richard C. Marohn to conclude that Hardin had a narcissistic behavior disorder? There are numerous signs and symptoms of narcissistic personality disorder, and the severity of symptoms vary. Here are just a few. People with the disorder can have: (1) exaggerated sense of self-importance; (2) a sense of entitlement; (3) expect to be recognized as superior; (4) belittle or look down on people they perceive as inferior; (5) take advantage of others to get what they want; (6) an inability or unwillingness to recognize the needs and feelings of others; (7) be envious of others and believe others envy them; (8) arrogant behavior; (9) trouble handling anything they perceive as criticism; (10) react with rage or contempt and try to belittle the other person to make themselves appear superior.[4]

Other factors to consider are too much or too little parental control. In John Wesley Hardin's case, his father displayed very little control and made excuses for his actions. There was probably a lack of parental empathy during childhood and too much expectation. The Reverend Hardin wanted John Wesley to follow in his footsteps and preach the Gospel. When he went the other way, he enabled him. Other factors are genes. Personality disorders like narcissistic could also be genetically inherited. If you have a narcissistic parent, it is possible that you could turn out to be narcissistic. Finally, recent research has identified abnormal brain structures in people with NBD. Apparently, Dr. Marohn based his diagnosis on some or all of these mentioned factors. However, many of us are narcissists. We have a sense of ourselves; we can be selfish, vain and arrogant. Few of us, however, have enough traits to combine into the kind of narcissistic behavior and extent of lack of empathy where alarm bells start to ring, and six guns are blazing fire upon those who get in the way.

In his letter, Teagarden gave a somewhat different view of Hardin's behavior. In his letter to Mollie he wrote, "I knew the heart and soul of John like the daily companion and implicitly trusted friend from childhood to manhood. We spent our time together in the woods, hunting and fishing, and in sports, when we were not required to be in school or at Sunday school."

Teagarden went on to talk positively about Mollie's grandfather, the reverend James G. Hardin, educator, attorney, minister, and circuit rider. Teagarden and John Hardin attended school in Sumpter, a large town at the time, located on the beef trail to Alexandria. In the same class for a number of years, they started with the learning of the alphabet. Under various teachers they both continued in the same class and the same desks until they passed through the highest classes of that seminary, ten or eleven years later.

Teagarden went on to say, "John, in all his actions in and out of school, was candid and honorable, as he was throughout this life."

Teagarden claimed John enjoyed perpetuating practical jokes on other students and even the teachers. When questioned, he would confess readily and accept his punishment. "He protected me from harm many times from other boys," said Teagarden.

Once, Teagarden claimed he was unjustly blamed by the teacher who was approaching with a hickory stick to punish him. John Hardin stood up and moved in front of the teacher and had a knife in his hand. He told the teacher that he would kill him if he touched Teagarden. The teacher retreated, "and that was the end of it because everyone knew that John Wesley Hardin meant what he said," wrote Teagarden. From adolescence to manhood, Hardin and Teagarden had a very close relationship.

Teagarden continued in his letter to say, "It is therefore true that no one knew the inwardness of John's character as I did. There was not in his life or character a single sordid or dishonorable motive. All men who treated him fairly and decently were met more than half-way, but those who, by mistake or preference, treated him wrongfully or disrespectfully always had their challenges accepted, and they usually got what was coming to them."

Then, Teagarden wrote a paragraph justifying John's killing of the ex-slave Maje in 1868, indicating it was just and acceptable in those days to kill a black man after being assaulted by him. Teagarden made no mention of Hardin's difficulties in Navarro County a year later; probably because Hardin never wrote about them and probably never told anyone.

In 1869, John Wesley Hardin's father sent him to the Pisgah Ridge Community, Navarro County, Texas, to hide out from the law with his Dixon kin. On August 26, 1869, the Grand Jury of Navarro County, charged John Hardin with assault with intent to murder Mr. S. H. Presley. It was noted that Hardin "Used a six shooting gun to shoot, with intent to kill, one S. H. Presley.

A Mr. W. H. York was a witness to the shooting. Hardin had fled the county and a reward may have been posted. He was never arrested for the crime. The *Dallas Daily Herald,* dated September 1, 1877 reported: "The *Statesman* thinks the reports of Hardin killing twenty-seven men are false. It hints at records and rewards for but few charges. He is indicted for murder or assault with intent to kill in eleven counties: Freestone, Grimes, Titus, Hill, Hopkins, Sabine, Trinity, Comanche, Wilson, Gonzales and Navarro."

In his letter, Teagarden told Mollie that everyone hated Governor Davis's dreaded state police and every time one was killed people applauded. He went on to claim that no one was ever indicted for the killings. Then, he wrote that John had trouble with some gamblers and bullies and, "first and last had to shoot two or three."

He believed any decent man could get along with John without any trouble and so could any man who treated him fairly. "He was always honorable but frank in his manner and would not brook any kind of insult from anyone, His sensitive, resentful disposition would not stand for it. Those conditions caused all of John Wesley Hardin's troubles," wrote Teagarden.

Teagarden criticized irresponsible writers as lying blowhards who told false stories about John and magazines featuring false and sensationalized stories about him on more than one occasion.

He went on to tell Mollie that someday he would take up the long-neglected duty and write the true story of John Wesley Hardin's character. He never did and he probably never dreamed of his letter from almost eighty-eight years ago, being used today to re-visit one of Texas most notorious gunfighters.

Chapter Four

The War on the Texas State Police: John Wesley Hardin and His Conflicts with Authority

By Chuck Parsons

This story was first published in Central Texas Historical Association. *Reprinted with permission.*

The life and career of Texas desperado John Wesley Hardin (1853-1895) is fairly well-known by professional historians as well as western history buffs. He has been the subject of one motion picture, although it was never well received by the public, and numerous articles of varying quality. He is known for the most part because of his autobiography, written after his release from prison and then published posthumously in 1896. As one would expect he presents himself in very different terms than how nearly everyone else viewed him. At best he was an unreconstructed rebel, being too young to fight in the Civil War, but made up for that during the years following the war's end. If he had been a few years older he may have experienced enough violence on the battlefields so that when the war ended, he could become a peaceful farmer or preacher, as his parents had hoped he would become. His autobiography has been kept in print with inexpensive reprints as well as a printing by the University of Oklahoma Press.

A number of biographies have appeared since that 1896 publication of his *Life of John Wesley Hardin, as Written by Himself*, and to a great degree they have depended on his chronology although some have gone far beyond a mere recital of his gunfights. The biographies by Richard C. Marohn, Leon Claire Metz and most recently this writer along with Norman Wayne Brown all attempted to research into records originating from the Adjutant General's office, documents the Fifth Military District as well as other records and contemporary newspaper accounts. We will not attempt to discuss here his problems with law officers other than those who belonged to the Texas State Police, whether regular policemen or Special Policemen. Many writers do not make a distinction between the regulars or the specials, but they were not the same. One prime distinction was that the specials were confined to their own county whereas the regulars had a fairly large district to work in. Hardin himself, however, considered any type of policeman his potential enemy.

The Texas State Police as a history has been well researched and written by two scholars of the first order: Barry A. Crouch and Donaly E. Brice. Their research was published in 2011 entitled *The Governor's Hounds: The Texas State Police, 1870-1873.*[1] Whether John Wesley Hardin ever thought of the policemen wearing a badge indicating he was a bona fide policemen is unknown, but he certainly had no respect for them. Much of his autobiography discloses his racial attitude towards the force — as it was made up of whites, blacks, mulattos as well as Mexicans. That the force was the first law enforcement body which bore no discrimination charge was lost on Hardin as well as many other Texans who had a built-in prejudice for any person other than white southerners. Hardin's life story is filled with examples of his antipathy against the former slaves who now had their freedom as well as a high degree of authority.

An idea of Hardin's attitude towards Governor Davis's police force is expressed when Hardin first visited his cousins the Clements brothers in Gonzales County in early 1871. "E. J. Davis was governor then, and his State Police were composed of carpetbaggers, scalawags from the North, with ignorant Negroes frequently on the force. Instead of protecting life, liberty, and property, they frequently destroyed it. We all knew that many members of this State Police outfit were members of some secret vigilant band, especially in DeWitt and Gonzales counties. We were all opposed to mob law and so soon became enemies."[2]

Hardin thus became an enemy of the force as a whole, not with any particular member. When writing his life story he was conscious of how he wanted posterity to remember him, thus many incidents are quite different from the actual event as recorded by contemporary records. When in prison he had many opportunities to write to family members in which he was not concerned with posterity, but only a justification of his actions. Most telling is his statement in a letter written to his wife on June 24, 1888, a decade after the beginning of his incarceration. In this letter he wrote (with his spelling left intact):

> I belong to no man or Set of men[.] I belong to my Self to my god[.] his Laws are Right[.] It has been Said of my [sic] before I reached my majority that I had vanquished E.J. Davis's police force from the red river to the rio grand from matamoris to Sabine Press that I had defeated the diabolical Burero agents and U S Soldiers in many contests.[3]

Just who claimed that he had accomplished these remarkable feats is not stated, but apparently that idea had been expressed to him that he was a mighty warrior waging war against the Davis police force. Hardin wrote his autobiography describing incidents in which he engaged in a great number of life and death gunfights, ending up killing or wounding former slaves, U.S. Soldiers, Indians and Mexican vaqueros on the cattle trail to Kansas, State Policemen, Texas Rangers, Pinkerton detectives, almost any type of lawman or individual who challenged his being. After each killing or gunfight in which the man may have been only wounded, Hardin felt it necessary to justify his action: it was always a case of defending himself against someone wanting to kill him or deny him his liberty, or his honor.

In May 1874 in Comanche County Hardin killed a deputy sheriff from Brown County who attempted to arrest him. This resulted in quick retaliation by citizens from Brown and Comanche Counties. The "mob" as Hardin viewed them, failed to capture Hardin but did arrest his brother and two cousins. They were quickly lynched without even the semblance of a trial. Two other cousins were shot to death resisting arrest.

This was totally a new and dangerous situation for Hardin, as he realized he had to leave Texas; he fled to Florida to live with relatives of his wife. Finally, in 1877, Texas Rangers caught up with him in Pensacola, Florida, arrested him and delivered him back to Texas for trial. He was tried, found guilty of second-degree murder and sentenced to twenty-five years in the penitentiary at Huntsville.

Hardin was anything but a model prisoner, but after a number of unsuccessful escape attempts and savage beatings he realized cooperation was a far better policy. His efforts to obtain a pardon was successful and resulted in his release in 1894. During those sixteen years spent in prison he wrote numerous letters to family members and friends and most importantly contemplated how he wished to be known by posterity. As one might expect his life story is one of justification for every act; each act was one of defending his life or property or honor. As one reads *The Life of John Wesley Hardin* one might come to the conclusion, he was an innocent victim forced to become a freedom fighter, resisting the oppression and the tyranny of the E.J. Davis police.

Hardin was certainly not the only young man who resisted the presence of Federal authority occupying Texas. In the aftermath of the traditions of southern society being overturned much violence resulted. Now there was increased violence by whites against blacks, even blacks against other blacks and blacks against whites. Seemingly the fear of raiding parties of Comanche or Kiowa was reduced with the increasing violence in the so-called civilized communities of Central and East Texas.

Republican Governor Davis now by mid-1870 had created the State Police, an organization which was intended to reduce the amount of violence. From the beginning there was resistance, not only by Davis's political adversaries but by those who resisted authority in general. John Wesley Hardin resisted and developed a reputation as one who greatly resisted Davis's force, but from the record did Hardin wage a greater war than numerous others. Cullen Montgomery Baker created terror in the northeast while William Preston Longley developed a reputation as a killer of freed slaves in Central Texas.[4] These remain the two best known, after Hardin. Does Hardin deserve the reputation which history has given him?

The Texas State Police was organized in 1870 with the first

four captains selected by July of that year. Of the four captains Hardin experienced differences with two: Leander H. McNelly whose station was at Burton in Washington County, and John Jackson "Jack" Helm whose station was in Concrete, DeWitt County. Helm was also the sheriff of DeWitt County.

Hardin in 1870 for a while lived with his uncle, Robert Hardin in Washington County, near county seat Brenham. During the day much of the time was spent helping with the farm work; at night he and his cousins of about the same age traveled into Brenham for enjoyment. On one occasion their horses were stolen, which they did not report to the authorities, nor did they ever recover the stolen horses.

He remained with his uncle, "until the crops were laid by" but he realized "the country was getting pretty hot for me." The heat was caused by Captain McNelly and his police force. Hardin explained that he and his uncle "on consultation with friends" convinced him to move on, although one suspects the real reason was that McNelly was aware of his presence and Hardin did not want to face McNelly, a tough man who had served four years fighting for the confederacy and — as later events would show — believed in quick punishment for wrong doers.

Early in 1871 Hardin had his first "difficulty" with the State Police. At Longview Hardin was arrested, the police believing he was responsible for the death of a policeman in Waco, although this was one killing of which Hardin was innocent. After being initially jailed in Marshall two men were selected to deliver him to Waco: Lieutenant E. T. Stakes and Private James Smalley of the State Police. After crossing the Trinity River Hardin managed to obtain a weapon and killed Private Smalley while the lieutenant was gathering fodder for the horses. Hardin recalled this incident happening in January 1871. The exact date was January 22, 1871, and this was the first state policeman Hardin killed.

The contemporary press provided a fairly complete recital of the events leading up to the death of Private Smalley. First printed in the *Fairfield Ledger* of January 28, it was reprinted in *Flake's Daily Bulletin* of Galveston. Apparently, there were two others involved which Hardin conveniently overlooked in his telling of the incident, and from those two and Lieutenant Stakes additional details were learned. In addition to the alleged Waco killing, Hardin was accused of having stolen the horse he was riding. When Private Smalley was alone with the prisoner, he "drew a repeater and shot Smalley through the back, and as Smalley turned and attempted to draw his own pistol he was again shot in the abdomen and fell," whereupon Hardin fled the scene on Smalley's horse.[5]

For Lieutenant Stakes who was in charge, to allow a prisoner to obtain a weapon, then kill one of his guards and then escape on the private's horse at the very least the event proved to be one of poor management, or poor training, if there was any. The police records fail to indicate that the state provided any special training for its men. Lieutenant Stakes, however, who had joined the force October 14, 1870, remained in the force until his resignation on December 19, 1871.[6]

Hardin then returned to his father's place where he soon decided it would be best if he lost himself in Mexico. He explained that somewhere between Waco and Belton he was arrested "by men calling themselves the police" while asleep. He identified the trio as Smith, Jones and Davis. The trio intended to deliver their prisoner to Austin, but somewhere near Belton they stopped for the night. Instead of guarding their prisoner carefully the three consumed their whiskey and then fell asleep themselves. Hardin, who had remained sober and alert, obtained their weapons and killed the three. He then "took an oath right there never to surrender at the muzzle of a gun."[7] This is Hardin's version of his second encounter with members of the State Police.

If Hardin did kill three men somewhere in Bell County at this time, they were not members of the State Police, regardless of Hardin's belief. Although there were members of the force named Smith, Jones and Davis none were killed or even wounded according to the record. Hardin may have killed three men during this period; by identifying them as police he allowed his readers to further appreciate how he, this unreconstructed rebel David, took on three Goliaths and conquered them, impressing his readers even more than if he had simply killed an unknown person.

In Hardin's account he again returned to his father who provided no admonition on his son's conduct but instead encouraged him in his wandering life and even went part of the way to Mexico with him. Or so Hardin wrote. He may have accompanied him but probably not very far; the son was on the run.

He continued on his way to Mexico, but then stopped in Gonzales County to visit his cousins, the Clements brothers, who apparently he had never seen before. The Clements were cattlemen and were busy gathering their herd to go to Kansas and sell. Fugitive Hardin forgot about his trip to Mexico and joined them, becoming an inexperienced drover. For the next few months Hardin was in less danger than previously as he was relatively safe while on the trail.

He experienced adventures going through Texas and the Indian Territory, found excitement in Abilene, Kansas, and then returned to Texas. He made no mention of visiting his parents after an absence of nearly a half year, but he went to the Clements where he again encountered the presence of the Texas State Police.

Hardin explained how he had his first confrontation with police in Gonzales County. Many considered efforts of the state to enforce the law were actually the result of "mob law" and were openly opposed to it. What initiated the violent resistance was when "a lot of Negro police made a raid on me without legal authority. They went from house to house looking for me and threatening to kill me, and frightening the women and children to death."[8]

Two special policemen, Green Parramore[9] and John Lackey[10] found Hardin at a small grocery store in southern Gonzales County. They did not know Hardin by sight, but in that small building they announced to everyone they were there to arrest him. Possibly they saw his weapons and intended to arrest him for that infraction. They ordered him to throw up his hands "or die!" and then demanded the pistols he wore. Hardin deftly pretending to comply drew both pistols, first surrendering them but then flipping them so the barrels pointed towards Parramore. Hardin knew better than to submit to arrest and shot Parramore.

"Down came the Negro, with his pistol cocked," and he then

saw another policeman outside on a white mule. Since with
Parramore dead, Hardin now focused on the other, wounding
Lackey in the mouth. There was no bravery in John Lackey that
day. To escape Lackey ran to the nearby Smiley Lake and dived
in. Hardin wrote: "I afterwards learned that he stayed in there
with his nose out of the water until I left."[11] Hardin placed this
battle in September 1871.

This was Hardin's version in which he described how the
police, after frightening the women and children on a raid to his
place, then attempted to arrest him without legal warrants. He had
to resist of course and kill in what would be self-defense. Governor Davis did not see it that way and on November 5 signed the
proclamation offering a reward of $400 for Hardin. After the usual
preliminaries the proclamation continued: ". . . it has been made
known to me that on or about the 18th day of October A.D. 1871 in
the County of Gonzales . . . one Green Parramore was murdered by
one Wesley Clements, alias Wesley Hardin . . . and is now at large
and a fugitive from Justice." In spite of his reputation the reward
would be paid only upon Hardin being arrested and delivered to
the sheriff of Gonzales County inside the jail door.[12] The term of
"dead or alive" would come soon in reward notices for Hardin.

In Gonzales County the news of Hardin's killing a policeman, even though he was a "special" which made no real dif-
ference except to record keeping in the Adjutant General's office, "spread like fire" as Hardin recalled; then he and friends
"declared openly against Negro or Yankee mob rule and misrule in Gonzales."

Hardin recalled that friends of Parramore and Lackey, who
had both been killed as believed by some, threatened to raid the
Sandies area and "with torch and knife depopulate the entire
country." If we accept this then we must also accept Hardin's
response, that he gathered about two-dozen men "good and
true" and sent word that they should come on "that we would
not leave enough of them to tell the tale." Some others already
advised the group to disperse. Then Hardin claimed that "from
that time on we had no Negro police in Gonzales."[13]

There were two threats acting against peace and calm in
Gonzales County in the period following the killing of Parramore. In Austin Governor Davis seriously considered declar-

ing martial law in Gonzales County in an effort to quell the disturbances. The *San Antonio Herald* first reported that Gonzales County "narrowly escaped martial law" and further reported that friends of Parramore and Lackey, believing that both had been killed by Hardin, "assembled in numbers, armed, and wanted to go after the bodies of their comrades." If this had happened there would have been more violence as they would have had to go into the dangerous area where Hardin and his friends frequently assembled. Sheriff James T. Mathieu and Gonzales Mayor Ezra Keyser prevented their involvement with any action against Hardin or recovering the body of Parramore.[14]

John Lackey no doubt found some comfort and perhaps medical attention in his community; who did recover Parramore's body is unknown and where he was buried is also unknown, but perhaps in the southern end of the Gonzales City Cemetery where there are a number of Lackeys buried. There is no separate marker for John Lackey, however.

After this dramatic incident Hardin apparently avoided trouble as in his narrative he recalled nothing happened of significance except attending the marriage of Jim Clements and Anne Tennille. At the time Hardin was courting sweetheart Jane Bowen and soon they were married. Hardin had heard that the police might pay the wedding a visit, but they "would have met with a warm reception in those times, when the marriage bells were ringing all around."[15]

Hardin may have thought that by this time the police had learned to leave him alone, but if so, it was not because they were afraid of him: rather he had no difficulties with them as he was temporarily out of the country. Hardin spent some time going down to the King Ranch, for what reason is unknown, and then spending some time in Nueces County before returning to Gonzales County.

Once having rushed home to his bride Jane it was time to think of business, and this not so strangely led him into another difficulty. His business was gathering of horses to drive to a market in Louisiana. He hired men named Harper to do the actual driving while he went on ahead and spent some time visiting relatives, they all agreeing to meet at Hemphill in Sabine

County. The brothers Jesse and John Harper may have been experts at driving horses, but another reason for Hardin choosing them to handle his herd is that their father, Elmer (or Elmore) Harper, was sheriff of Sabine County then.

Even though a sheriff was officially a member of the State Police, the fact that his sons were working for Hardin perhaps allowed him to "look the other way" in this situation. As a county sheriff, Harper certainly was aware of who Hardin was, and may have decided that since the fugitive had done nothing wrong in his county, he would overlook the matter. Hardin frequently made friends with law officers even though he was a hunted fugitive.

There were no problems on this trip to Louisiana, except at Hemphill, where he should have merely met with the Harpers and continued on, without his urge to gamble. The situation was one in which he made another man's difficulty his own.

As Hardin recalled, a traveler from Louisiana on his way home to Austin, was arrested for carrying a pistol. William Connor was his name, although Hardin called him "O'Connor" and legally as a traveler he had a right to go armed. However, State Policeman John Henry Hopkins Speights (identified as "Sonny" Spites by Hardin) did arrest him and he was fined $25for the offense.

When Hardin learned of this he was "outraged" and somehow managed to get a new trial for Connor at which he was acquitted. In the meantime, Speights had confiscated the horse and pistol from Connor. At this point, a young boy began to taunt Speights for his conduct in arresting a poor traveler resulting in him threatening to arrest the boy and at which time Hardin entered into the situation.

Speights threatened to arrest him as well for interfering with a police officer, and Hardin responded he could not arrest "one side of me."

Speights, by now frustrated with the situation began to draw his weapon, not realizing how dangerous the situation had become and not knowing who his adversary was. Hardin, a two-gun man, drew his weapons now having the duty to defend himself, a derringer and a six-shooter. Hardin wounded Speights in the shoulder and Speights ran. Hardin gloriously informed his readers at this point that he "would not shoot a fleeing man, not even a policeman," so he left the scene and went to the Harpers. It was fortunate for Speights that Hardin's aim was poor that day, as the running policeman only had a shoulder wound from which he recovered.

It is possible that Hardin did not want to kill the policeman, being in the town where his friend was the sheriff. That is basically Hardin's version and this time fortunately Speights wrote or had written for him his version. His original letter has not survived but it was summarized in a ledger preserved among the adjutant general's papers. Hardin recalled the incident happening on July 26, but it was later as the report from Milam, Sabine County, was dated August 21, 1872.

> [Policeman Speights] Reports operations & states [he] arrested one Wm. Connor, for carrying a pistol & turned him over to civil authority & states he was shot & wounded by Wesley Hardin, and boasted of him being the 8th policeman he had shot & killed & that he (Speights) was the only one he did not kill & states Hardin is still at large although the sheriff followed him but came back without success & states there were two men [who] assisted him in getting away, Wm Harper & Ferguson, a discharged policeman.[16]

Eight policemen Hardin had shot and killed, or at least shot but not killed? Who were they? Jim Smalley would be the first; killed in 1871; then for the sake of Hardin's count we can figure in Smith, Jones and Davis also in January 1871; Green Parramore in Gonzales in 1871; and later he will claim three policemen from Austin in September 1871.

The total adds up to eight but by the time he made the boast the killing of three policemen from Austin had not happened. Since the killing of Smith, Jones and Davis at best could only be three individuals but not policemen, we must discount them. In truth it would appear from available records that Hardin, even though waging a war on the State Police, only killed two and wounded one.

It is not surprising that William Harper assisted Hardin in his escape. He was a son of the county sheriff and in mid-1872 he was nineteen years of age. He was probably acting out of friendship, coupled with working for his father with the horse herds which Hardin would soon sell to them. Elmer Harper, although classified as a farmer on the 1870 census, was appointed county sheriff on March 29, 1871, was elected November 8, 1872 and served until October 6, 1874.[17] In 1860 his family consisted of he and his wife Julia and six children, of whom William was seven.[18]

"Billy" Harper, as Hardin recalled him, reached to where Hardin was hiding out about evening that day and reported that Speights was only wounded in the shoulder but "scared to death. He said everybody approved of what I had done."[19]

Hardin parted from Sabine County, after selling the horse herd to the Harper brothers, and then continued on his wandering life, and perhaps looking for a new adventure. The new adventure came in an unusual source: he was actually assisted in escaping from a gunfight by a former State Policeman, Jeremiah Alexander Ferguson.

There was a discharged policeman named Ferguson, but it is difficult to determine just why he assisted Hardin in escaping — but according to Private Speights' report that is what he did. If he and William "Billy" Harper both helped Hardin one might conclude the discharged policeman and Harper were friends, and Ferguson was helping out a friend. Or Ferguson may have been dissatisfied with his former superiors in the Adjutant General's office and in a small way gaining some satisfaction in helping Hardin.

Jeremiah Alexander Ferguson, a one-time Texas State Policeman who later assisted the wounded Hardin. *Courtesy Charlotte Pool.*

J. A. Ferguson had joined the force on September 19, 1871, but was discharged October 31, 1871, a very brief time in the service. Nothing has been found to explain why he chose not to continue in the force. In the late war Ferguson had served in Company F of the 11th Texas Infantry. Sheriff Harper had also served in this unit and possibly a friendship developed during that time. But for whatever reason, Ferguson, a former State Policeman, assisted Hardin in his escape from Sabine County.[20]

The Adjutant General was required to complete an annual report for the governor.[21] He included in his 1872 report the number of policemen killed or wounded or who died since the beginning of the year of 1871. The number of policemen killed was eight, two of them by Hardin. Jim Smalley was killed January 22, 1871, at Marshall; Green Perrymore was killed October 19, 1871, at Gonzales. Of the five wounded there were John Lackey, October 19, 1871, and J. H. H. Speights, wounded in August, 1872, at Milam. Two policemen died of natural causes, W. M. Speights, the father of J. H. H., May 17, 1872, at Milam.

Thus, if one were to look at the casualties, of the fifteen men listed, four of them were the result of Hardin either killing or wounding, nearly one fourth, which is strong evidence that Hardin was waging a war on the State Police.[22]

In addition to the casualties of the police force, Britton included a very important paragraph on the status of the state, and although he did not mention the name of Hardin in this aspect of his report, one can almost feel that Hardin was on his mind when preparing it:

> Lawless bands of armed men depredate continually throughout the State. The lives of the peaceful, law-abiding citizens were constantly in danger. The strong arm of the military government (when in power) could scarcely keep in check the well-organized bands of desperadoes roaming through the State. Local authorities, in most instances, were absolutely powerless; and in many cases, through fear and intimidation, under control of the desperadoes themselves. Sheriffs, who would, otherwise, dare not make arrests, having no means of securely holding

prisoners when arrested.[23]

The last adventure with the State Police nearly cost Hardin his life. The incident happened in Trinity City in what became a costly incident for Hardin in blood and money began at the John Gates Saloon. Hardin and an individual named Philip Allen Sublett, began their rowdiness playing ten pins. Of course, plenty of drinking was done by both parties and an argument erupted as to something in the game. Tempers grew heated, but then cooled, but then Sublett disappeared, only to return with a double-barreled shotgun. Hardin was severely wounded by the blasts of Sublett's weapon. But, Hardin managed to chase him but could inflict no damage. He had the satisfaction of "making the coward run."

Through friends Hardin managed to get away from Trinity and found some safety and medical attention, ironically back in a hotel in Trinity City. With good medical attention Hardin was able to be moved, two of the buckshot having been removed from his back. He then was moved again, as it was rumored police were searching for him. Actually, a trio of police did discoverer where he was hiding out, but in the subsequent gunfight one of the policemen was killed. This is another example of a killing which may have occurred, but little contemporary evidence exists to support it.

Finally, fully realizing he was in a desperate situation, wounded, unable to travel and depending on friends to move him from place to place, and not in his home country where he had numerous friends to protect him, Hardin now decided to become a prisoner of the law rather than taking chances on the State Police or a mob to catch him and probably kill him without benefit of a trial.

He managed to communicate with Sheriff Richard B. Reagan of Cherokee County, that he would be willing to surrender to him. The surrender was made, and Sheriff Reagan traveled to Austin with his prisoner where Hardin was placed in the Travis County jail. After additional time for his wounds to heal, Hardin was transferred to the Gonzales jail. State Police Sergeant L. C. Lock and a three-man detachment delivered their prisoner safely to Gonzales.

Although there are no Gonzales newspapers extant for this period the delivery did receive coverage in other journals. The *San Antonio Herald* noted: "Joe [*sic*] Hardin, less than twenty-one years of age, has been arrested in Cherokee County in this State. Joe is said to have killed twenty-four men in Texas and four in Kansas, and to be the son of a Methodist preacher."[24] Obviously there are errors in that report, but it does substantiate Hardin's recollection.

Sergeant Lock turned Hardin over to Sheriff William E. Jones in Gonzales. Hardin now became Jones's problem, and being well aware of who his prisoner was and realizing he had many friends, he was concerned over his responsibility. He wrote that court had adjourned and "nothing can be done until the next term which will be in February 1873. Recommends the removal of Hardin from Gonzales as the jail is not secure."[25]

Indeed, the jail was not secure for someone like Hardin; on November 20, Jones had to write another letter to Austin, stating that Hardin had made his escape from the jail the night of November 19, and that he had offered $100 for his arrest. Jones certainly knew of the much bigger reward already offered for him, but did he make this token of an effort to save face?[26]

Although there were dozens of other young men who had issues with the Republican administration in Austin in general and the State Police in particular, most did not actively engage in combat with the police. More commonly was sending letters to a local or area newspaper, such as the *San Antonio Herald* or *Galveston Daily News,* telling of perceived atrocities of the police. Generally, the focus of misrule by the administration or the police was that the force was made up of "ignorant negroes" but actually at most the force was about thirty-three percent black and a lesser degree of Mexican with the majority white.

Even though Hardin's life story has been kept in print for over a century and most writings are based primarily on that source, much of it can be regarded as truthful due to the historian reinforcing his claims with other contemporary documentation, such as official records in the Adjutant General's office. The basic facts are substantiated, although there is virtually no drama in the reports summarized in the ledgers of that office.

A pistol believed to have belonged to John Wesley Hardin. *Courtesy Ronnie Atnip.*

But, in considering the sources now available, one must conclude that John Wesley Hardin was waging a war on the State Police, although he may not have been conscious of that at the time.

Years later during the sixteen years spent in prison, he had ample time to reflect on his past and may have then concluded that he had been a warrior, freedom fighter fighting the oppression and tyranny of the occupying Federal forces and the State Police of Governor E. J. Davis.

During the feuding days John Wesley Hardin visited Taylor cousins located eight or nine miles south of Bonham, Texas, at Taylorville. He was known to place hideout guns around where he stopped. One was left in a chicken coop and not taken with him upon leaving. It was discovered but not removed, thinking he may come back for it. The coop finally rotted to the ground and a family member retrieved the pistol.

In his autobiography, Hardin tells of the fight he had with Mexican cowboys: "The pistol I had was an old cap and ball, which had so much play between the cylinder and barrel that it would not burst a cap unless I held the cylinder with one hand and pulled the trigger with the other."

He also mentions Jim Taylor as a cousin. The pistol was identified as a Confederate copy of the Colt-Eli Whitney, 2nd Model, Navy Revolver. Same pistol used to kill those Mexicans?[27]

Chapter Five
Deputy Sheriff Charles M. Webb's Last Gunfight

By Norman Wayne Brown

This story was published by *The Tombstone Epitaph* July 2021 issue. The editor changed the title to *John Wesley Hardin's Last Notch*, Actually, Hardin would go on to escape to Florida for over three years and would kill again and again.

Charles M. Webb has been a web of mystery ever since researchers started looking for his pedigree. Interest in Webb started only after his death in Comanche, Texas. He was a deputy sheriff of neighboring Brown County and was killed in a gunfight by the notorious John Wesley Hardin and his desperadoes. The gunfight took place in the street, outside a saloon in Comanche. A number of theories surround the motive behind the killing of Webb, as well as who he really was, his family, and his origin.

When Charles M. Webb was shot dead on May 26, 1874, his body was taken back to Brown County and buried in the Brownwood Greenleaf Cemetery. It was late in the day when his body was claimed in nearby Comanche and probably buried the next day. Webb was a member of Brownwood Masonic Lodge No. 279 and annual return for 1874 lists him as an Entered Apprentice. Webb was probably of the Baptist faith being his grandfather was a Baptist minister. There was no Baptist church located in Brownwood until two years after Webb's death. Noah T. Byars became a Baptist missionary in 1842. He founded the First Baptist Church in Brownwood in 1876 and lived there until his death in 1888. He is also buried in the Masonic section which he donated.

Later, a group of "Daughters of the Confederacy" decided Charles Webb had served in the Civil War and erected a marker at his gravesite. This was possibly because a Charley Webb was listed as having served with Quantrill's Raiders. That was the only reason the group decided he was one and the same. This was highly unlikely that it was this Webb based on two factors; his young age and the fact that he was living in Kentucky from birth in 1848 until 1870 or later.[1]

Finding his home state was difficult as there were literally hundreds of Charles M. Webb's during those years with over one hundred located in Texas alone, per federal census of 1870. But none had a birth date even close to his. In addition, no record of him having served in the military during the Civil War exists. Therefore, the Civil War marker at his gravesite provides a false and misleading link to serving in the Civil War.

Reverend Charles Webb had a son named Hamlet L Webb and he married Catherine R. Asbury on February 24, 1847, in Cynthiana, Harrison County, Kentucky. Hamlet and his brother, Charles Webb Jr., owned and operated a mercantile store in Cynthiana. On August 2, 1848, Hamlet's wife, Catherine, gave birth to a son, and he was named Charles M. Webb. Charles had an uncle, Reverend Isaac Monson and that could have been Charles' middle name, however, there is no written evidence to support the theory.

Hamlet's wife, Catherine, died April 11, 1849, and was buried in Indian Creek Baptist Church Cemetery in Cynthiana. After she passed away, Hamlet realized he could not take care of a small child, so Charles was given to paternal grandparents, Charles and Elizabeth Webb. The 1850 federal census of Nicholas County, Kentucky, lists Reverend Charles Webb, age seventy-eight and Elizabeth Davis Webb, age sixty-eight, both from Virginia. Charles M. Webb is listed in the household, age one.

Previously, it was erroneously theorized that thirty-year-old Huldah [sic] Webb, in the same household, was the mother of Charles. Actually, Huldah was single and was Charles's aunt and she died of consumption in 1852. Charles remained with his grandparents until his grandfather, Reverend Charles Webb, died on April 1, 1853. Charles was then taken back by his father who was still widowed and living with brother, Charles Jr., and his wife, Mary Cook Webb. Then, Hamlet remarried in 1854 to

Elizabeth E. Long and they made their home in Cynthiana.[2]

Charles Webb remained with his father and stepmother until the early 1870s. The federal census of 1860 lists Charles at age twelve with personal estate valued at $1,200. That could have been in error as it was uncommon for a minor to own personal property. The 1870 census lists Charles still in the household, single, age twenty-two, with occupation of farmer. His father remained in the mercantile business. Sometime after the census was taken, Charles packed his kit and headed west, settling in Brown County, Texas.

Charles M. Webb was on the tax rolls in Brown County as early as 1873 and became a lieutenant in the Texas Rangers from January to the end of March 1874, serving in Captain James Connell's company. They were disbanded due to lack of funding by the state. Almost immediately, he was hired as a deputy sheriff of Brown County.

A Texas Ranger in Captain John R. Waller's Company A, Frontier Rangers and years later a member of Major W. M. Green's Texas Ex-Ranger Association, wrote an article in the May 1924 edition of *Frontier Times* and told what he believed led to deputy Webb's demise. Marshal Jeff Green and Deputy Sheriff Charles Webb killed a Hardin gang member named Charlie Davis, yet another member escaped. He was Jim Baird.

Afterwards, Deputy Webb arrested Baird along with Jim Buck Waldrip, a rancher, and both were convicted for cattle stealing and sent to prison. Therefore, John Wesley Hardin and his associates wanted to kill both Webb and Green. A horse race was allegedly staged which in those days, always drew a crowd from miles away and they believed Deputy Webb would attend, to which he did.[3]

Deputy Webb probably had no idea what John Wesley Hardin looked like, nor would he have known Hardin's companion, Jim Taylor, or his Dixon cousins, as they were all new to the area. Regardless, they met in front of the saloon. According to Jim Taylor, John Wesley Hardin was drunk, and Taylor claimed he grabbed Webb after he pulled his pistol and spun him around three times to spoil his aim. He then claimed that it was he who killed Webb.

The actual truth of exactly how it went down may never be known. When Hardin was tried and convicted for the murder, he was not allowed to take the stand to tell his version of the shooting. He received a twenty-five-year prison sentence in Huntsville, Texas. While in prison, Hardin in a letter to his wife Jane, stated "I killed Webb in self-defense." Ironically, John Wesley Hardin, son of a Methodist Preacher, killed Charlie Webb, the grandson of a Baptist Preacher.

Another version of the Hardin/Webb showdown came from a Brown County official who remained anonymous. He visited with a reporter in June 1874 and claimed to be an eyewitness to what he called "a cold blooded murder" in Comanche that occurred on May 26, which caused retaliation from the citizens of Comanche and Brown counties. It was declared an uprising. Charles M. Webb, a deputy sheriff out of Brown County, was the victim and the men who took part in his killing were John Wesley Hardin, two Dixon cousins of Hardin, and Jim Taylor who was unknown and unnamed by the eyewitness.[4]

It was common knowledge, or at least the belief, that the killers of Deputy Webb were part of a band of cattle thieves who had been operating their rustling for a good while in that area. The thieves were not going unnoticed as twelve indictments had been made against them and Webb had been instrumental in arresting three of the gang. Of those three, two were in custody in the Georgetown jail and one had been released on bond.

The eyewitness stated that Hardin and associates had waited for Webb in a saloon and when he entered, they started an argument with him. Two faced him in a defense stance while the other two moved to the side, indicating they planned to do him harm. Observing this, Webb backed away to the outside of the saloon as the gang followed.

After they were in the street, they again parried off as before and started drawing their six-guns. Webb outdrew them and fired rapidly, but the eyewitness claimed Webb's shots went wild, when in fact, Hardin was hit in the side. Hardin was the first of the gang to return fire, followed by the two Dixon cousins. The fourth gang member was not mentioned. He was Jim Taylor, a close friend of Hardin. Webb fell to the ground when the first shot hit him in the neck, but he raised himself to his knees and fired two more shots at his assassins before taking rounds to his hand and abdomen. Then he fell dead to the dusty street in front of the saloon.

The county sheriff and several people had reached the scene by this time, as Hardin walked up to the sheriff and handed over his pistol and said, "Take that and then take me if you can."

The sheriff ordered someone at the scene to watch and guard Hardin while he disarmed the others. They did not resist and gave up their guns without a problem. However, during that time Hardin had slipped away, mounted his horse and fled the town of Comanche. Henry Ware fired four shots at him as he fled but didn't hit him.[5]

This killing marked the end of John Wesley Hardin's gang. In the following days a manhunt by citizens and Texas Rangers combed the region in search of the gang. Joe Hardin, Tom and Bud Dixon, would be placed under arrest only to be hanged by a mob. Two other cousins, Ham Anderson and Alexander

Charles M. Webb grave marker in Greenleaf Cemetery, Brownwood, Texas. A small marker was added to indicate Webb had served in the Civil War. That was not true. *Norman Wayne Brown Collection.*

Bible record of Charles M. Webb's parental grandparents Charles and Elizabeth Webb of Kentucky. *Courtesy Dianne Webb.*

Barekman were later killed. Other members of his gang would eventually be lynched.

John Wesley Hardin sent his first cousin, J. D. Hardin to Kansas to sell his cattle and bring him the money to aid in his leaving Texas. Some historians believed that J. D. was John's little brother Jeff D. Hardin, but it was John Dixon Hardin who made the trip. A few years later, after leaving Texas for Florida, Hardin was captured after a night of drinking and gambling in Pensacola, Florida. He and friends had boarded a train's passenger car at the train depot while planning to return to his wife in Alabama. After his capture and return to Texas, he was tried and convicted.

It is unclear why deputy Charles M. Webb left the farm in Kentucky. The family had a lot of children around the kitchen table come feeding time. That may have been a factor. He may have just wanted to be on his own and shed fatherly authority or maybe he got into some kind of difficulty that caused him to pack his kit and head for Texas. It is unknown if or how many gunfights Charles Webb had been in but when he met the notorious and deadly John Wesley Hardin that day in the dirt street outside that saloon, it became his last gunfight.

A family legend was passed down about this author's great grandfather as follows: As a young man he had to flee his home state after the Civil War for thinking he had killed his abusive stepfather. He was asked some years later by a grandson, "Grandpa, why did you go to Texas?"

"Well son," he replied, "that's what you did back then. When you got in trouble, you went to Texas." But that's another story yet to be told.

Chapter Six
John Wesley Hardin's Capture

By Chuck Parsons

This story was one of the chapters in *A Lawless Breed, John Wesley Hardin, Texas Reconstruction, and Violence in the Wild West* (Denton: University of North Texas Press, 2013). *Reprinted with permission.*

> Jane I am in good hands now they treat me Better than you have any Idea and assure me that I will not be mobed . . . Jane Be in cheer and don't take trouble to Heart . . . But what I have done in Texas was to Save my own Life [.]
>
> *J.H. Swain, August 25, 1877*

On the afternoon of August 23, 1877, Mr. John H. Swain was ready to leave Pensacola and return home to Jane and their three children. He was seldom alone on these ventures as a gambler, and this afternoon he was with several friends who together boarded the train, going into the smoker car. They may have been doing more than gambling, as they placed their shotguns above their heads in the baggage racks. Had they been hunting?

What the other passengers did not know was that even with their shotguns out of reach, Mann and Swain had at least one pistol on their person; possibly Hardy and Campbell carried one as well, but not openly.

The "peaceable Mr. Swain" and his companions, James Mann,[1] Shep Hardy[2] and Neil Campbell Jr.,[3] now settled in for the train ride. So far as the community knew this quartet was not of any importance to anyone, had never caused any trouble, and any gambling they did was more for enjoyment than any other reason. They chose this car as Mr. Swain had now taken up smoking a Meerschaum pipe, which he now readied to light up.[4] There may have been a few other passengers in this smoker; if there were his

smoke would not be considered a bother by them.

As county sheriff, Wil-
liam H. Hutchinson[5] made it
a practice to walk through the
cars prior to the train's departure. He may have considered
this action nothing more than
a part of his job. He expected
no trouble but if there were
any "undesirables" present he
would have them removed.

This afternoon he entered
the smoker, but none of the
passengers thought anything
of it as they knew this was a
common practice of his.[6] And
the quartet knew him, if not
as a good friend, at least as a
friendly acquaintance. Today,
Sheriff Hutchinson, known to

John Wesley Hardin as he appeared in
1875 in Florida. *Courtesy Robert McCubbin
Collection.*

many as "Hutch," entered the car, but today his deputy A. J. Perdue[7] was with him as well. This caused no concern to anyone.

The pair of lawmen addressed Mr. Swain. Hardin recalled that
Perdue now asked him if he could not stay over in order that he
could win some money back he had lost at the gambling tables.
Hardin demurred, explaining that he would like to but not then,
as he had other business to attend to, adding, "Business before
pleasure I can't stop over."

After all, he had a wife and three small children waiting for
him. Hutchinson and Perdue now exited the car, knowing that
their target was there and off guard. Hardin was in the forward
section of the car, facing the rear. He had his arms stretched out on
the back of the seat, James "Jimmy" Mann next to him. Hardin had
his pipe in his mouth, and all were relaxed.[8]

Now the figure of Ranger John B. Armstrong darkened the
doorway and in his left hand he held his cane and in his right hand
he held a Colt revolver with a seven-inch barrel. At the same time
he entered the rear, Hutchinson, Perdue and William D. Chipley

Train at the Pensacola depot circa 1877 and could be the train that Hardin was captured in. *Norman Wayne Brown collection.*

entered the opposite end of the car, all four descending on the man with the Meerschaum pipe in his mouth.

Almost immediately Hardin saw the Colt revolver, and knew this was no casual action. "Texas, by God!" he yelled out, later explaining that this "smelt of Texas business." With that recognition he attempted to draw his pistol, but now three men grabbed his arms, his legs, and he struggled. He attempted to draw his weapon but due to a flare up of an old wound he did not wear a gun belt and holster, but concealed under his shirt, suspended, a sort of shoulder holster. Violently he struggled, yelling out "Robbers! Protect me!" but with his arms and legs held down his struggles were useless.[9]

James Mann reacted as if there were robbers on board and whereas Hardin could not get his pistol in operation, Mann could. He fired at Armstrong, narrowly missing his head. Armstrong returned the fire and shot Mann through the heart. Even though fatally shot, Mann was able to get off the train and onto the depot platform. Here other deputies had been stationed, and they fired at him as well. There Mann died, not knowing why the attack had occurred or who had killed him.[10]

Now Armstrong had reached the struggling group. Even if he had wanted to shoot Hardin, it would have been too dangerous. He ordered Hardin to surrender, threatening to shoot if he did not, to which demand Hardin replied, "Blow away. You will never blow a more innocent man's out, or one that will care less."

Another version of his response was "Shoot and be damned. I'd rather die than be arrested."[11]

Hardin continued to fight, and to stop his struggles Armstrong hit him over the head with his Colt, knocking him out. The reward had been for Hardin "dead or alive," but Armstrong wanted to take this prisoner back to Texas alive. There are numerous accounts of the capture of Hardin, but all agree on one salient fact, the law had captured John Wesley Hardin. In spite of denials of his true identity, the prisoner maintained his name was Swain.

Once "Swain" was subdued Armstrong pulled the bell cord which was the signal to start the train and pull out of the Pensacola depot. James Mann was left dead on the platform; Hardy, Campbell and "Mr. Swain" were in custody, the latter in irons. What Armstrong and the others perhaps now realized, with them entering opposite ends of the car, and knowing there would probably be gunfire, did they consider the possibility that they could be shooting at each other?

One of them could be hit by what is today known as "friendly fire." And Hardin himself, once conscious, may have begun to

A view on Pensacola's Palafox Street in 1876. This is where John Wesley Hardin did his drinking and gambling before his capture at the train depot. *Chuck Parsons collection.*

The Pensacola Depot, 1878. Chuck Parsons collection.

realize that even if he had gotten his pistol out, he would have had no chance to survive with that number of lawmen acting against him. He had been in a capture or death situation.

After some miles the lawmen stopped the train and allowed Campbell and Hardy off, as they had no reason to keep them. Hutchinson and Perdue now were informed as to who Swain really was and Armstrong offered them $500 for their assistance. Just before Whiting, Alabama, the train stopped again to allow Chipley and Duncan off to search for Brown Bowen. They would meet Armstrong in Whiting, with or without Bowen.

On the next day, August 24, Armstrong and Duncan with their prisoner reached Montgomery. The exhausted lawmen placed Hardin in the jail and they checked into a hotel to get some needed rest. On the 25th, at Verbena, Armstrong sent another telegram to Adjutant General Steele, in which he expressed confidence that all was well and they would soon get to Austin with the most wanted man in Texas: "It is all day now [.] on our way [.] papers O K[.]"[12]

At Montgomery they had learned a mob waited which intended to take their prisoner away; somehow Duncan had learned of this and had avoided this mob. At Decatur, Alabama, some 140 miles north of Verbena, they allowed the prisoner to write a letter to his wife. Armstrong apparently had obtained some stationary, in this case the letterhead of attorneys at law, J. S. Clark and David P. Lewis, and, presumably, with the cuffs on, John Wesley Hardin wrote to Jane. At the top he scrawled a note to Allen Marion McMillan,[13] asking him: "I Hope [you] will consider Janes circumstances and Help Her all you can", in other words, help him with the three young children and in any other way he could. His letter began:

My Dear Wife and children this is the first time that I

have had an opportunity of writing you a letter Since I was arrested in pensacolia [sic]. Jane they Had me foul yes very foul I was Sitting im the Smoking car Neal C [Campbell] & poor (Jimmie M) [Mann] By my Side with my arms Stratched [sic] on the Side when they came in. 4 men grabed [sic] me one by each arm and one by each Leg so the[y] Stratched me locking and quick. But poor Jimmie he Broke to run out of the cars and was Shot dead by some of the crowd on the out Side.

Hardin, obviously aware that these Rangers wanted to take him back to Texas alive, attempted to assure Jane he would be safe and also to console her for her additional responsibilities in her raising the three children alone. He had to have known that he would have to stand at least one trial and that could take months. He continued:

Jane I am in good Hands now they treat me Better than you have any Idea and assure me that I will not Be mobed [sic] and that when I get there that the Governor will Protect me from a mob and that I will hav[e] the Law [.] Jane Be in cheer and don't take trouble to Heart But look to the Bright Side [.] Jane I have not murded [sic] any Body nor Robed [sic] anyone But what I have done in Texas was to Save my Life [and] Jane time will bring me out[.]

He then explained to her that he had been able to have an attorney the previous day and attempted to be released on a writ of *habeas corpus* but the Rangers were able to show the proper papers for his arrest, convincing the judge he was indeed John Wesley Hardin, and thus was not released. His letter continued:

Jane I got a rit of Habas corpus [sic] yesterday But fail[ed] to get out my trial was Set for Tuesday but a requisition come for John Wesley Hardin Last Night So they Saw & Swore that I was the man J.W. Hardin that Killed Web[b] of Comanchie Texas So they Had to give me up[.] Jane be cautious in writing me for they will examine your Letters before I see them & Direct your letters to Austin texas to J H Swain[.]

The drawing of the actual arrest as interpreted by artist R. J. Onderdonk. This drawing first appeared in Hardin's *Life*.

Now he attempted to give her further assurances that this particular trial will not last long, and she should feel confident that
the day will come when they are together again. He continued:

> Jane they can Never Hang me nor penitenchry [*sic*] me
> for Live [*sic*, life] by Law times are not like they was
> when we left Texas [as] Mob law is played out Jane I
> expect that it is a Good thing they caught me the way
> they did for they had Forty men with the Shariffe and
> Deputie of pensicola So you See I would have been a
> corps [*sic*] Now instead of Being a prisoner if they Had
> not Stratched me as they did [.] Jane I had no Show to
> get my pistol if I Had I would Have Been Killed [as] my
> Hands were caught the first pass[.]   Jane I am in Good
> Hopes yet – write to me at austin Texas[.]

And now he took the opportunity to explain to Jane why he
was captured when he was:

> Jane Brown's Bad conduct caused me to get caught me
> in Pensacolia and all so his Last Letter to Texas Stateing
> that his sister Joines Him in Sending Love to all[.] the
> Detective was Boarding at N B [Neill Bowen's] When

the Letter came an[d] watched them put the Letter away and then Stole the Letter out N.B. thought the man Mr Williams to be a merchant wanting to rent the Store House[.]

And now Hardin knew full well who his captor was:

But His name is John Dunkan [*sic*] a State Detective of Texas[.] Jane B. [Brown] is the cause of my arrest. Jane go to your F [father] as Soon as possible and then You can come to See me if You wish do not Give up where there is a will there is a way [and] Remember 1874 & 1872 So Good By my Dear Wife (You Hav[e] ever Been True) remember me to the children and also to all my friends and do the Best You can[.] Tell you[r] connection your circumstances So Good By Dearest one[.][14]

He signed it "J. H. Swain." No doubt the "1874" and "1872" refers to the chaotic life they led following the Comanche tragedies; 1872 may refer to the crisis of Hardin being so severely wounded by Phil Sublett and the subsequent arrest and being jailed in Gonzales, and his escape.

Also, on the twenty-fifth of August, the day Hardin wrote that letter to Jane, the press issued a telegram datelined Whiting, Alabama. It was reprinted not only in numerous Texas newspapers but also in the *Atlanta Constitution*, the *Chicago Tribune*, and the *New York Times*. Of the extensive newspaper publicity Hardin received, this telegram received the greatest circulation.

Whiting, Ala., August 24 – To-day [*sic*] as the train was leaving Pensacola, Florida the sheriff, with a posse, boarded the cars to assist two Texas officials to arrest the notorious John Wesley Hardin, who is said to have committed twenty-seven murders, and for whose body four thousand dollars reward has been offered by an act of the Legislature of Texas. His last murder in Texas was the killing of the sheriff of Comanche County. He has lived in Florida for years as John Swain, and being related to county officers, has escaped arrest. About twenty shots were fired in making the arrest. Hardin's companion, named Mann, who had a pistol in his hand, was killed.[15]

Although there were a few
minor errors in this news report,
the name of John Wesley Hardin of Texas was spread across
the land. Armstrong, Duncan,
Hutchinson — none was mentioned by name.

Hardin recalled that there
was one opportunity for him to
escape, but the sharp eyes of the
detective from Dallas prevented
it. He gave the place as Decatur,
Alabama, when they were to
change the cars for Memphis,
Tennessee, and possibly it was
there. He wrote that his guards
"were kind to me, but they were
most vigilant. By promising to
be quiet I had caused them to

Texas Ranger John B. Armstrong as he
appeared in the 1870s. *Courtesy the Armstrong Family.*

relax somewhat, and they appeared anxious to treat me kindly,
but they knew their life depended on how they used me."

Hardin thought it was in Decatur where they stopped to
change cars, got rooms and ordered meals. When their meal arrived Hardin asked that his cuffs be removed. "Armstrong," he
wrote, "unlocked the jewelry and started to turn around, exposing
his six-shooter to me, when Jack jerked him around and pulled his
pistol at the same time. 'Look out,' he said, 'John will kill us and
escape.'"

Hardin laughed at them both, ridiculing the idea, but he almost managed to get a pistol and perhaps have shot one or both
of the Rangers. This is what Hardin wrote.[16]

Duncan recalled that it was somewhere in Arkansas that he
saw Hardin had a knife up his sleeve, but "I took it out and threw
it out of the car window. Then, John Wesley Hardin broke down
and cried. We told him to behave himself and we would get along
all right, and then he asked us if an attempt was made to lynch him
would we give him a pistol to defend himself with." The answer
was that he would be armed, and that he would not be mobbed.[17]

Sheriff William Henry Hutchinson, Sheriff of Escambia County, Florida. *Chuck Parsons Collection.*

On August 27, the train carrying Hardin crossed into Texas and arrived in Austin the next day. Hardin was placed in the new Travis County jail, fortunately not the old one which had caused such a public outcry that caused the new one to be built.

As Hardin was on the train rushing back to Texas he certainly was concerned for Jane and the children and their immediate welfare, but what of brother-in-law Brown Bowen? He had no real idea of how much help Allen Marion McMillan could give them, and he could not expect Brown to be of much help either.

One wonders if his feelings against Brown were now stronger than his concern for Jane's welfare. It was now known that Bowen was a fugitive from Texas as well. One newspaper report provided an interesting word picture which may hold some facts, but portions are definitely fictitious. A Montgomery reporter described that a woman, "with a child six weeks old" had come up from Pollard on August 26, and "represented herself" as Mrs. Hardin.

Some of what was written was accurate, that she was the daughter of a "gentleman" named Bowen, that she had married Hardin about six years before, they had three children, and that she was present when Webb was killed, meaning she was in Comanche, but not at the street when the killing took place.

She told the reporter that she intended to get back to Texas "as soon as possible" but had little hope of seeing him again as he would probably be killed before he ever got to Texas. She also said two other men, "Dickerson and Taylor," were "engaged" in the shooting which resulted in Webb's death.

The reporter must have misunderstood her when he wrote that "both of whom were caught and hung by the Rangers" as it was only Dixon hung, along with his brother and brother, Joe Hardin. Certainly, Jane knew that, so we must blame the reporter for this misinformation.

"This woman," continued the reporter, "has the bearing and converses like a person of much more than ordinary nerve and courage. She boasts of being able to shoot and manage a horse as well as most men and says things will be made extremely lively for Armstrong and Duncan . . . and also for some others who had a hand in the capture of Hardin."

She may have actually made these threats, or the reporter may have added them for dramatic effect. Jane Hardin was described as "twenty-one or twenty-two years of age," and "seems to be very well educated and speaks fluently, expressing her feelings with much force."

Jane may have seemed "very well educated," but it is difficult to determine much about that aspect of her being, apparently the letters she wrote to her husband while he was in prison have not survived so it is impossible to comment with any degree of accuracy about her formal education. Probably it was no more than a rudimentary education, unlike her husband's whose father was a teacher as well as a minister.

The reporter concluded with this amazing statement, that in Texas, "she has a good competency, consisting of a fine plantation well stocked, given her by her father on his marriage to Hardin."[18]

Neill Bowen may have had some acreage to farm, but he had no plantation.

Whereas Armstrong and Duncan had only the responsibility of delivering their prisoner to the Travis County jail, what of the men who were involved in the capture who were left behind? Sheriff Hutchinson had a dead man laying on the train platform. Presumably the body was carried to the city morgue and the family notified. He also was obligated to give at least a big thank you to the twenty or more deputies he had arranged to be on the station platform to assist as needed, although for the most part they did nothing except several may have shot at Mann as he left the train car. Armstrong had shot him, but reportedly he had received numerous balls once outside of the train car. Hutchinson had been promised a portion of the reward, and he certainly obliged himself to give part of it to deputy Perdue, and perhaps divide some of it among the other deputies.

William D. Chipley continued with his working with railroads, providing and improving transportation for the Panhandle. This Georgia native was born June 6, 1840, the son of a prominent physician and Baptist minister. He received a superior education, and in 1858 graduated from Transylvania University in Lexington, Kentucky. After joining in 1861 Company C of the 9th Kentucky Infantry, by 1863 he was a 1st Lieutenant. He was wounded in the Battle of Shiloh and was again wounded and cap-

William Dudley Chipley who helped in Hardin's capture. *Chuck Parsons Collection.*

tured by the army of General Sherman at the Battle of Peachtree Creek at Atlanta.

He spent the duration of the war as a prisoner. In 1876 he moved to Pensacola and took charge of the Pensacola Railroad, and with his success and vision by the 1880s he was general land contractor for the Louisville and Nashville Railroad. He continued in public life, elected mayor of Pensacola, and in 1894 elected to the Florida State Senate. He had lived a full and exciting and purposeful life, dying on December 1, 1897. On the public square in Pensacola is an obelisk erected in his honor; the name of the county seat of Washington County was changed to Chipley.

Hutchinson continued in law enforcement for one more term, re-elected in 1880 but after the second term chose not to run again. His career was not nearly as full as Chipley's had been. At war's end he never formally surrendered, but merely went home. He married in 1868, but their first child died the following year. In 1882 his wife died after fourteen years of marriage. He remarried on February 20, 1884, in his hometown of Prattville, Alabama, to Miss Ila Temple Merritt, and on December 15, 1884, their daughter,

Lily Kathleen, was born. In his later years he became active in local politics, serving on the Board of Public Works, the United Confederate Veterans, and the International Order of Odd Fellows. On
September 27, 1906, a hurricane wiped out his fishing business,
leaving him nearly destitute. Hutchinson died at his home on January 14, 1911.

Hutchinson's name, nor that of Deputy Perdue, was mentioned in Hardin's autobiography, only the names of Armstrong
and Duncan. As most of what has been written about Hardin is
based on Hardin's *Life,* those two Florida officers have been large-
ly ignored.

Although not mentioned by name, Hutchinson's action may
have guaranteed the success of the capture. Hardin himself said
he was at the point of getting his pistol when the man seized him,
thus saving Armstrong's life. Although there was a large reward
offered for Hardin's capture, how much was divided up among
those involved in the capture remains to be determined.

Armstrong or Duncan may have promised them $500, but
they certainly did not have that with them when they arrived in
Pensacola. Whatever oral arrangement or promise was made, and
how much was actually paid, Hutchinson was not satisfied. On
September 6, 1877, he left for Austin to discuss with Texas officials
the disposition of the reward. The *Dallas Herald* reported his trip
was for the purpose of arguing "his claims for a division of the
reward offered by the state for the arrest of John Wesley Hardin."

The *Herald* quoted a telegram it had received from Hutchinson: "I captured and forwarded John Wesley Hardin, the noted
Texas outlaw. Please telegraph me amount of authoritative reward
offered." The *Herald* indicated that Hutchinson was probably "left
out" as Armstrong and Duncan had already drawn the $4,000 re-
ward. If this was true, no official record of the reward being paid
to anyone has been located.[20]

Years later, shortly after the August 19, 1895, death of Hardin,
Hutchinson wrote a lengthy letter to the *Dallas Herald* in which he
gave his account of the capture. He began his letter pointing out
that the official version as printed in the newspapers about Hardin's life and capture was "so strongly at variance with the actual
arrest, that at the insistence of many friends" he was advised to
furnish the details of Hardin's capture.

Hutchinson claimed that he met the Texas officers at the state line as they had "lost all trace of Hardin." He had then telegraphed his deputy, A.J. Perdue, "who has since died, who was as brave a man as ever lived" and who notified him that their man was there in Pensacola. In this version Hutchinson claimed that he and Perdue entered the car together, and that the sheriff knew who Hardin was. Hutchinson brushed past Hardin, then "suddenly wheeled" and said, "I believe I want you."

Hardin replied, "D –n you, take that" and struck Hutchinson "in the lower part of the abdomen with both heels, from the effect of which up to this date I have never recovered."

As Hardin sprang up Hutchinson struck him "across the face with a pistol." He and Perdue then seized Hardin, and in the process discovered Hardin had a pistol concealed between his shirt and undershirt.

Hutchinson grabbed the pistol, tearing the shirt, "and tossed it out into the car." Up to that point the struggle was Hardin against Hutchinson and Perdue alone, but needing more, the sheriff called to Mr. John E. Callaghan[21] who quickly responded and together they subdued Hardin and tied his feet together with a rope.

Then, still according to Hutchinson's version, J. W. Mann "becoming badly frightened" jumped up and attempted to escape through an open window, and "while in the position of leaping, was shot from the outside of the car." Then, and not until then, Armstrong and Duncan entered the car.

With their prisoner, Armstrong and Duncan, with Hutchinson and Perdue, headed north. After a few miles the sheriff instructed his deputy to turn the prisoner over to the Texans at the state line, "which was carried out to the letter in an orderly and quiet manner, shaking hands in parting from Hardin and telling him he regretted the necessity of arresting him." At this point Hardin supposedly remarked: "I have killed twenty-seven men, and Hutch, you came near being the twenty-eighth."[22]

This is a remarkable version of the arrest, and it is strange that for eighteen years Hutchinson kept his anger within, only expressing this after Hardin's death. Why did he not communicate this to the Dallas newspaper, or any Texan newspaper, within the months or the year following the capture?

It would be very interesting to know what Hardin would have

said in response to it. Hutchinson obviously believed Armstrong and Duncan cheated him. He admitted he knew nothing about the trip back to Texas, but "out of the promised rewards, aggregating several thousand dollars, I was the recipient of a paltry $500, which was given to those assisting me in the capture outside of Lieut. Armstrong and Duncan."

How much accuracy there is in these lines is difficult to say, and one does suspect that by 1895 Hutchinson had brooded over his part in the capture and selfishly felt he ought to have received more of the reward than he did. Perhaps through the years his actual participation in the arrest became blurred to the point that he and Perdue alone accomplished what in reality was a combined accomplishment of the four. Even if one were to dismiss the entire Hutchinson version of what happened that August twenty-third, we do learn that Deputy A. J. Perdue had passed on, no longer able in 1895 to give his version of what happened that day.

Another question which now cannot be answered is that if Sheriff Hutchinson did know the real identity of the peaceable Mr. Swain, why did he not arrest him before the Texas officers came? If he had he, and presumably his faithful deputy, A.J. Perdue, would have had not only the reward but also the glory. The fact remains however that the wording of the reward stated that it was to be paid to whoever *delivered* Hardin inside the doors of the Travis County jail; this Armstrong and Duncan did, and Hutchinson did not.[23]

And what of Joshua Robert Brown Bowen? When he left Texas, thanks to Hardin and others liberating him from the Gonzales County jail, he fled to Santa Rosa County, Florida, some 600 miles east of Gonzales. In Texas the cattle industry dominated; in his new home area of the Florida Panhandle the logging industry dominated. Along with partner Sheppard Hardy the pair developed their own "industry" on the Styx River; logging for them may have been honest labor, or at times they stole logs instead of cattle and horses.

But Bowen did find time to court Mary Catherine Mayo and they were married in 1875, although no license has been located. Born in September 1858, she was seventeen-years-old when she tied the knot with this Texas fugitive. One son was born to the couple whom they named Neil, born in 1876 after Brown's father.

A wife and son did not change Bowen's lifestyle: rumors circulated that he had killed several men in Texas as well as Florida. Humorist Alexander Sweet of the Sweet & Knox team of authors referred to a "fatal misunderstanding in Florida" but paraphrased Bowen in commenting on it: "Although he had killed several men in Florida, he did not feel the slightest compunction. His conscience only troubled him about his Texas misdeeds. What happened beyond the state line was wholly immaterial to him."

Sweet knew how to turn a discussion of murder into a humorous comment, "This was the first time," he added dryly, "that I had heard of a man's conscience being affected by geographical boundary-lines."[24]

Bowen's undoing which was also Hardin's, was his row with Colonel Chipley. The *Pensacola Gazette* reported the argument, ending with Chipley taking Bowen's own pistol from him and then striking him over the head with it, as Chipley described the incident: "knocking him down and continuing his moral and healthy exercise until my weapon was spoiled and his head too. Bowen yelled for mercy . . . ."[25]

Chipley was a businessman to the core and five days following Hardin's capture he wrote Gov. Richard B. Hubbard of Texas urging he offer a reward for Bowen, in order that he (Chipley) could cover his expenses if it was necessary to follow Bowen any distance. Chipley anticipated Bowen would attempt to lose himself in southern Florida. He concluded, "Bowen tried to assassinate me while on my depot platform, a perfect stranger to him. . . . I nearly killed him at the punishment I gave him."[26]

Chipley concluded his letter pointing out that Lieutenant Armstrong had assured him that a reward would be forthcoming. In April that year the reward for Bowen was $350; on September 4, Hubbard telegraphed Chipley that the reward was now $500, delivered to the Gonzales County jail.

Armstrong, in his August 24, telegram to Adjutant General Steele, informed him "Have arranged to have Bowen captured" which presumably meant he and Chipley, and perhaps Hutchinson as well, were looking for him. Bowen had good reason to fear for his own continued liberty.

Bowen did not remain a fugitive for long. The Montgomery newspaper reported, while the news of Hardin's arrest was still fresh, "One of Hardin's supposed confederates was arrested near Pensacola Junction [September 17], and was sent to Texas in charge of Florida officials yesterday. He is the same man who made the attack on Col. W.D. Chipley several weeks ago."[27]

With Hardin and Bowen out of the country Escambia and Santa Rosa counties in the Florida Panhandle felt more secure in their homes. Sheriff Hutchinson was still alert however, as on October 26, he arrested Henry Sutton, reportedly Bowen's father-in-law, along with a man identified only as McCall. They were described as "chums of John Wesley Hardin." These arrests disposed of "the gang which has so long bid raw defiance hereabouts."[28]

On Saturday, September the first, 1877, the *Dallas Daily Herald* published a short paragraph that speaks volumes. It reads:

> Travis County-The Statesman thinks the reports of Hardin killing twenty-seven men are false. It hints at records and rewards for but few charges. He is indicted for murder or assault with intent to kill in eleven counties, as follows: Freestone, Grimes, Titus, Hill, Hopkins, Sabine, Trinity, Comanche, Wilson, Gonzales and Navarro. Lest an attempt should be made to liberate Hardin, a strong guard will be placed around the jail.—... The Comptroller issued Wednesday a warrant to Lieutenant Armstrong for $3,806, for the arrest of John Wesley Hardin, that being all the money left of the appropriation for this purpose. There is a balance of $194 due, which will be paid as soon as another appropriation is made.

Chapter Seven
Four Shots, One Kill

By Norman Wayne Brown

This story was published in *The Tombstone Epitaph*, November 2018 issue. Reprinted with permission.

> *"Hardin threw his hand on his gun, and I grabbed mine and went to shooting."*
>
> *Constable John Selman Sr.*

John Wesley Hardin was armed with two pistols, concealed in his hip pockets on the night of August 19, 1895. He entered the Acme saloon and began shaking dice with Henry S. Brown.

About 11:00 o'clock, John Selman and E. L. Shackelford entered the Acme Saloon to have a drink. They went to the far end of the bar. Hardin and Brown were at the other end of the bar, probably no more than ten feet away. Hardin, aware of the two men, watched Selman very closely.

"When Hardin thought my eye was off him, he made a break for his gun in his hip-pocket," said Selman. By instinct, Hardin's head surely turned toward the source of the threat. Selman pulled his gun and began shooting. "I shot him in the head first as I had been informed, he wore a steel breast plate. He fired three additional rounds at Hardin.

Deputy Sheriff J. C. Jones escorted Selman home and placed him under house arrest. He told a reporter, "I am sorry I had to kill Hardin, but he had threatened mine and my son's life several times and I felt that it had come to that point whether he or I had to die."[1]

This was Selman's version of how John Wesley Hardin met his violent death, made within hours after the shooting. If Hardin's back was turned why would Selman be concerned that he may be wearing a breast plate and go for a head shot?

John Wesley Hardin shortly before his death. A disputed photograph. *Chuck Parsons collection.*

John Selman, killer of John Wesley Hardin. *Chuck Parsons collection.*

There were numerous people in the Acme when the shooting took place, and several gave statements. What did Selman's friend Shackelford state?

"I heard shots fired. I can't say who fired and did not see it." Therefore, his statement had little value.

What did Henry S. Brown remember? "I heard a shot fired, saw a flash and Mr. Hardin fell at my feet at my left side. I heard three or four shots fired [and] when the first shot was fired Mr. Hardin was against the bar facing it, as near as I can say, and as near as I can say his back was towards the direction the shot came from." Hardin was facing the bar and Selman was to his left side at the other end of the bar. Therefore, his position was to the side and not the back.

What did R. B. Stevens, proprietor of the Acme Saloon see? "I was in the reading room." He did not see the shooting.

"Shorty" Anderson's explanation of what happened was very specific as he claimed he saw Hardin go for his pistol. "I saw Hardin turn and throw his hand back upon his hip, throw his coat back. Then I heard a pistol shot and he fell. Three or four shots were fired. When the smoke cleared up, I saw Hardin lying on the floor, and John Selman and his son in there." Note that Shorty saw Hardin turn toward Selman before the first shot was fired.[2]

Hardin was reputed to be the quickest man on the draw of all the Southwestern desperadoes.[3] But on this occasion, he was not quick enough if we accept the statement of witness Shorty Anderson. Too late Hardin had finally come to the realization that speed was useless against a man who already had his gun out, cocked, and ready to fire.

Adrian D. Storms, the El Paso County Attorney, kept notebooks concerning his business matters and on August 20, went to Thomas Powell's funeral parlor with two friends, Mau-

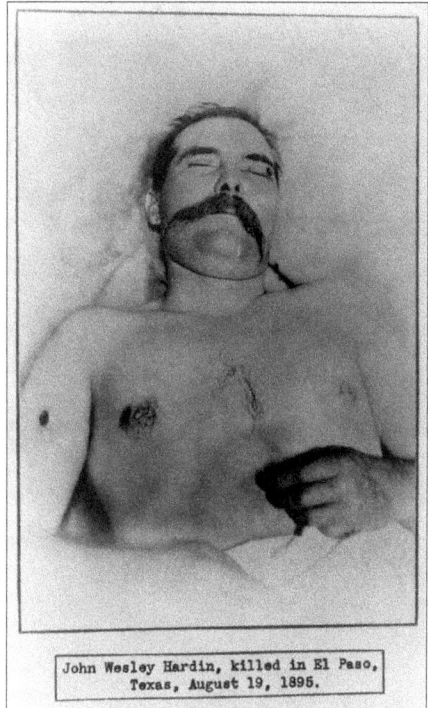

John Wesley Hardin, killed in El Paso, Texas, August 19, 1895.

This photo was taken of John Wesley Hardin two days after his death by photographer Bunge of San Antonio. *Chuck Parsons collection.*

rice McKillegon and Joseph Woodson, to look at the body of John Wesley Hardin. With a tape measure he noted: "Bullet hole in back of head was even in heighth [*sic*] with large cavity of right ear and 3 ¼ in[ch] from edge of rim of right ear. (A large cavity would mean an exit wound.) Bullet hole in left eye between eyebrow and edge of eye lid and at the extreme left of eye lid." (It reads that Storm may have been referring to two head shots. One to the back of the head and one to the left eye.)

Storms sketched in his notebook the brow, the closed eye, and the bullet hole, and continued: "Bullet hole just at right of right nipple where Powell said drs. said it went in. Another through right arm. Drs. said it went in back side. Therefore, Hardin was shot from back and front before falling dead to the floor.[4]

Hardin was killed on that night of August 19, 1895. Photographer J. C. Burge viewed the body later at the funeral home and

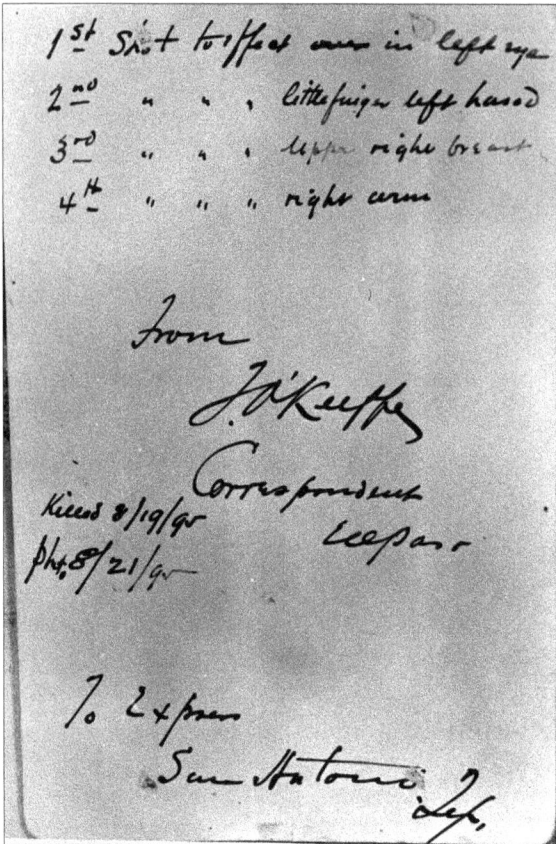

This is the reverse of the photograph taken by Bunge and he listed the entry wounds on Hardin's body. *Chuck Parsons collection.*

made at least one image of the deceased, showing the several bullet holes.[5] From the photograph one can see that one fatal bullet entered the left eye and probably went all the way through the skull to exit out the back of the head. Or did it? Burge wrote on the back of the photo: "1st shot to effect in left eye; 2nd shot to effect little finger on left hand; 3rd shot to effect upper right breast; 4th shot to effect right arm."

Therefore, according to Burge, one round from Selman's pistol entered Hardin through the left eye and may or may not have exited out the back of his head. Looking at the photograph, the wound to the left eye could not be an exit wound. An exit wound from a .45 caliber bullet would make a very large hole. A bullet entering the head expands upon hitting the skull and expands even more upon exiting the back of the skull. The wound to the left eye is, without doubt, an entry wound.[6]

The DA charged Selman with murder and the examining medical officer's version favors the DA and does not support the fact that the bullet hole next to Hardin's eye was small and neat, an entry wound. From examining the death photo and the testimony of witnesses it is clear that Hardin's body was not facing Selman, but his face did turn to receive the deadly bullet to the left eye. Storm noted that there was a head shot to the back of the head and the other to the left eye. While that is possible, it is most likely that only one shot went to the head, that being to the left eye and a large cavity exit at the back of the head.

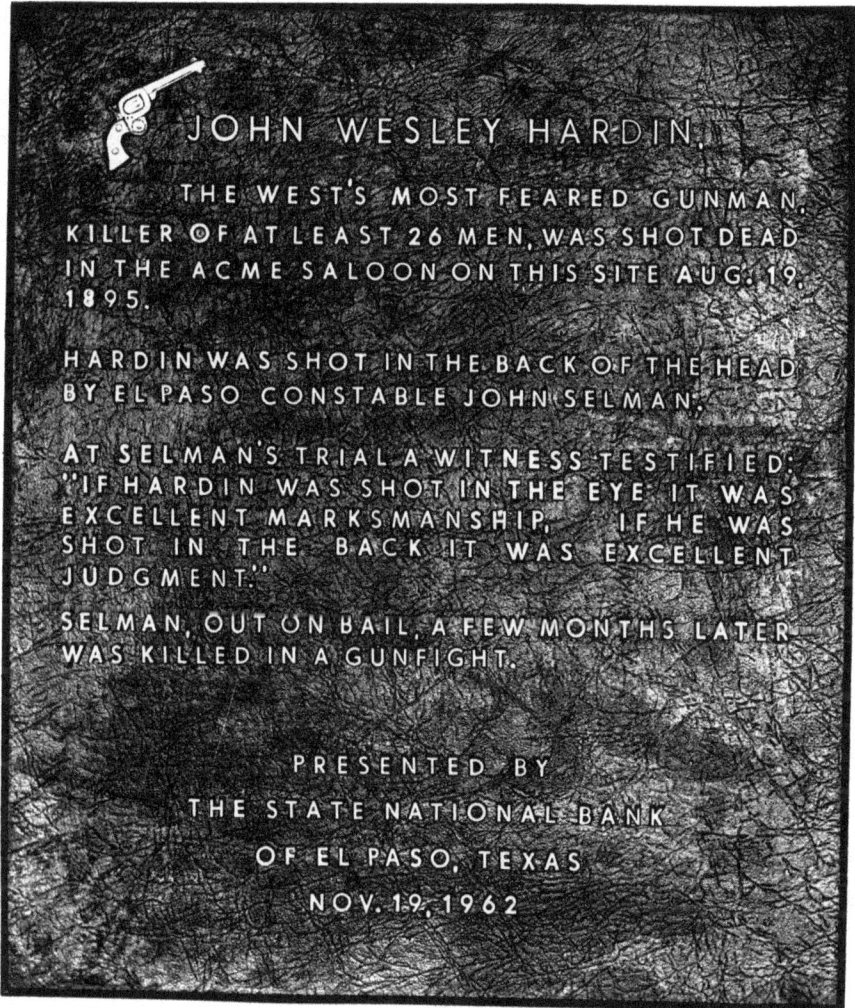

JOHN WESLEY HARDIN,

THE WEST'S MOST FEARED GUNMAN,
KILLER OF AT LEAST 26 MEN, WAS SHOT DEAD
IN THE ACME SALOON ON THIS SITE AUG. 19,
1895.

HARDIN WAS SHOT IN THE BACK OF THE HEAD
BY EL PASO CONSTABLE JOHN SELMAN.

AT SELMAN'S TRIAL A WITNESS TESTIFIED:
"IF HARDIN WAS SHOT IN THE EYE IT WAS
EXCELLENT MARKSMANSHIP, IF HE WAS
SHOT IN THE BACK IT WAS EXCELLENT
JUDGMENT."

SELMAN, OUT ON BAIL, A FEW MONTHS LATER
WAS KILLED IN A GUNFIGHT.

PRESENTED BY

THE STATE NATIONAL BANK

OF EL PASO, TEXAS

NOV. 19, 1962

This plaque is outside a business that is located in the spot where Hardin was killed by Selman. *Norman Wayne Brown collection.*

Chapter Eight

John Wesley Hardin's Brother, Gip

By Norman Wayne Brown

This story's original title was *The Life and Times of Gip Hardin*, published by *The Tombstone Epitaph*, February 2020 issue. Reprinted with permission.

The first time this author was ever locked behind bars was when employed by the Texas State Parole Board. On a warm summer day in 1984, the entry to the Walls prison unit in Huntsville, Texas, did not look inviting. Inside the lobby one is immediately faced with brass bars that prevent entry. When those bars swing open and one walks through, the bars make a distinguished bang when shut behind you, trapping you inside a prison; the same prison that housed John Wesley Hardin and his brother James Gibson "Gip" Hardin, many years before our time. Being locked up is not a good feeling until one becomes seasoned to it. This author worked behind the bars of many prison units in the Huntsville area for a number of years.

When the polished brass bars at the Walls prison unit in Huntsville, Texas, clanked shut behind James Gibson "Gip" Hardin, he probably figured his life no longer had purpose. Gip

James Gibson "Gip" Hardin, photo from Caffall-Clements family group so there is a degree of legitimacy about it. The image has been identified as Wes as well as Gip. *Chuck Parsons collection.*

had been in county jails for two years before arriving at the state pen. It seems Gip was foolish to do the same thing his big brother Wes did and that was to have a shootout with a deputy sheriff and win the fight but lose his freedom. When Wes killed deputy Webb, he received a twenty-five-year prison sentence and when Gip killed a deputy in Junction, Texas, he received thirty-five years but reduced to three years on appeal and new trial. His second-degree murder charge was reduced to manslaughter.

John Turman, hotel owner and deputy sheriff was killed in a gunfight by his friend Gip Hardin. *Norman Wayne Brown collection.*

Gip was born as James Barnett Hardin on August 15, 1874, at Mount Calm, Texas. Some years after his father's death in 1876, he changed his middle name to Gibson, the same as his late father. He then picked up the nickname of Gip. Because of this, many of today's historians decided Gip was short for Gipson and therefore changed Rev. James Gibson Hardin to James Gipson Hardin. While they were at it, they decided son Joseph Gibson should be Gipson and finally James Gibson would become Gipson as well. But those who made those changes erred as there never was a Gipson Hardin.

Gip obtained a teaching job in Junction in March of 1896. He became well known in the community as a good man and not violent like his brother John Wesley had been. He met and courted a young lady named Pearl Turner and they were married on January 17, 1898, in nearby Menard, Texas.[1]

On March 28, 1898, a number of people were having dinner at the Turman Hotel dining room with Gip Hardin being present. Some customers were discussing a trial and Gip started using foul language. John Turman was the owner of the facility and he stepped into the dining area and Gip continued to curse. John Turman was also a deputy sheriff of Kimble County, and he in-

structed Gip to take it outside. Gip did as instructed and once outside Deputy Turman grabbed Gip by the arm and announced that he was under arrest. This angered Hardin even more and he then threatened to kill the next man who touched him. As Deputy Turman and the friend attempted to grab him, Gip drew his pistol and opened fire, striking Deputy Turman four times. Deputy Turman returned fire twice but did not hit Gip. That was, on March 28, 1898. Deputy Sheriff John Turman was forty-years-old and survived by his wife Maggie and nine children. He had a lot of friends in Kimble County.

The next day, March 29, 1898, Gip was charged with murder of John Turman. He requested a change of venue for the trial and that motion also denied. Then on April 5, 1898, he requested a continuance and that was denied.

On April 5, 1898, Gip was declared guilty and sentenced to thirty-five-years in the pen. He appealed and that took a full year. Judge Wm. Addison took the bench and called the court to order and had Gip Hardin step forward. "Your request for an appeal has been upheld and the court has been ordered to move the trial from Kimble County to Gillespie County, Texas." The sheriff is hereby instructed to transfer Gip Hardin to Gillespie County jail prior to the September 1899 term.[2]

Gip Hardin was transferred to Gillespie County jail in Fredericksburg. He apparently was released on bond until his docket

Woodmen of the world donated the monument for the grave of deputy sheriff John Turman. Many of the prominent citizens of Junction and Kimble County were present, even the district judge was in attendance. *Norman Wayne Brown collection.*

date, and he was re-tried. This is based upon the birth of daughter Emma "Tase" Hardin, on September 6, 1900. His conviction for second-degree murder was reduced to manslaughter with a sentence of three years prison. Being he had been locked up for around two years, he had a short stay at the Walls unit where he was a schoolteacher for other inmates.

When Gip was released from prison he returned to Junction and reunited with wife Pearl. A second daughter, Varda was born on August 1, 1903. Things didn't work out between Gip and Pearl, so the relationship ended in divorce. Some sources claim he went up to Fort Worth and worked in the stockyards and when World War I broke out, Gip was hired to help deliver a herd of horses to the military in Europe. They were said to be off the coast of Florida when the ship got into a storm and Gip was crushed to death. For years historians could not prove or disprove Gip's death at sea.

Did the youngest son of Reverend James G. Hardin die in 1918 off the coast of Florida or did he die in some lonely and forgotten place at the end of a rope like brother Joe or shot to death like brothers John and Jeff?

Hog Island was a busy place with shipping companies and ship building. *Norman Wayne Brown collection.*

It was recently discovered that Gip did not die in an accident on the high seas. There is a place right off the coast of Philadelphia, Pennsylvania, named Hog Island. Gip was working for the International Ship Builders Company. On March 5, 1918, he was struck by a shuttle train on the island. He was taken to Methodist Hospital in Philadelphia and pronounced dead at the age of forty-three years, six months, and eighteen days. His sister, Nannie D. Witte, of Fort Worth, Texas, went to Philadelphia and arranged Gip's funeral. He was buried in Philadelphia's Mt. Moriah Cemetery. Everything on the death certificate was a match to James G. "Gip" Hardin.[3]

Twenty years and one month later, Gip's daughter, Emma Clarice "Tase" Hardin, a schoolteacher like her father, fell under a moving train in El Paso, Texas. Both legs were amputated at the

James G. Hardin's death certificate. The informant was Gip's sister, Nannie Wyatt, who later remarried. *Courtesy Mrs. Linda Rudd.*

knees, one arm was severed at the shoulder, and she had a fractured skull. Her death was ruled an accident. The date was April 25, 1938.

Gip's other daughter, Varda Hardin, married Jordan Anthony Clack who was a captain in the US Army. He died in 1964, at the age of forty-eight, while she lived until 1992. They are both buried in the Fort Bliss, Texas, National Cemetery. She was one of the few Hardins to die of natural cause.

Gip's prior wife, Pearl Turner Hardin, told the census taker in 1910, that she was a widow. She was probably embarrassed to say she was divorced. Pearl never remarried. She was born in 1881 and died in 1951, at age seventy, in Kerrville, Texas. She was laid to rest in the cemetery at Junction.

With the death of Gip, that closed out the lives of the Reverend Hardin's four sons who died with their boots on. After all, the old west was fading away.

Nannie Hardin Witte was the informant on her brother Gip's death certificate. Her photograph was among the personal items of John Wesley Hardin. The writing on the back of the photograph reads, "Mrs. Nan Witte, my good sister." Photo circa 1890s. *Chuck Parsons collection.*

Tase Hardin, daughter of James Gibson "Gip" Hardin, Texas death certificate. She was killed in El Paso, in 1938, and like her father, by a train. *Norman Wayne Brown collection.*

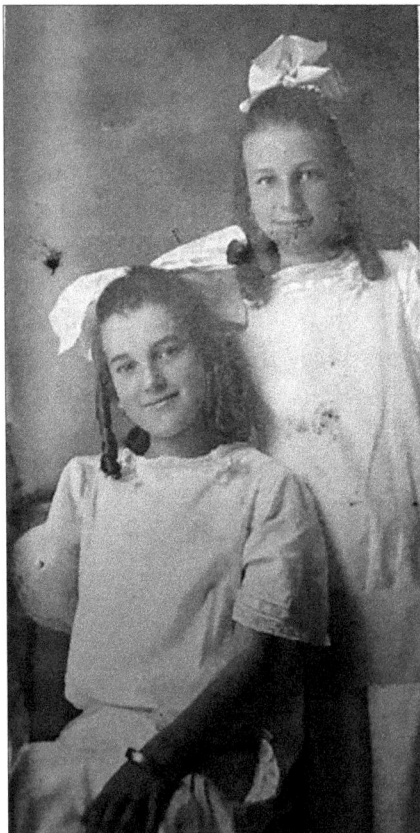

Gip and Pearl Hardin's daughters, Varda and Tase. *Courtesy Brenda Taylor Wade.*

Varda Yvonne Hardin Clack is buried in the National Cemetery at Fort Bliss, Texas. She was born in 1903 and died 1992. *Norman Wayne Brown collection.*

Chapter Nine
In the Shadow of John Wesley Hardin
By Norman Wayne Brown

This was the first article written on Jeff D. Hardin and published by *Wild West History Association Journal*, August 2011. Some information has proven to be in error. Chapter Ten provides corrections to those errors. *Reprinted with permission.*

The famous gunfighter and outlaw, John Wesley Hardin was a breed set apart from the average western man due to his quick and deadly nature with a gun. The habit got him in a peck of trouble on May 26, 1874. Hardin was celebrating his birthday in Comanche, Texas, when Brown County Deputy Sheriff Charles Webb drew on Hardin, a fatal mistake for Webb.

At the time, Hardin had a herd of cattle being held in Kansas and being in need of traveling money, sent his cousin, J. D. Hardin, not to be confused with his little brother Jeff D. Hardin, up the trail with instructions to sell the cattle and bring back the money.

Meanwhile, because feelings were high among revenge minded friends of Deputy Webb, the Hardin boys' parents, wife, brother, and cousins, were immediately taken into "protective custody." However, a group of Brown County men broke into the jail and hung Hardin's brother, Joe, and two of his cousins. As grass was later found between the victims' toes, it is claimed the ropes used were deliberately left too long in order to cause death through slow strangulation.[1]

Mary Lucinda Bundrant Barefoot was born in 1857, in Bastrop County, Texas. Her parents were Hardin and Nancy Bundrant and they moved the family to Gatesville, Coryell County, Texas, sometime between 1860 and 1870. She left her children a photograph, old memories, and a baffling story. Mary said as a young girl she was in love with a Hardin boy. The intensity of the relationship is measured by her saying, "He was my boyfriend, but my Daddy wouldn't let me marry him."

According to the family story, Mary was around seventeen or eighteen-years-old when she met the lad.[2] Moreover, according to Mary, her sweetheart was a brother of the gunfighter and outlaw, John Wesley Hardin, and the boy may have been Jeff Hardin. Her personal photo album was passed down to her children and grandchildren and remains in possession of family members today.

She may have told them his first name, but when someone wrote notes at the sides of a photograph in her old album, it read: "_____ Hardin, brother of John Wesley Hardin, later an outlaw."[3]

Of course, these family stories can become distorted and, in many cases, false, so the approach was guarded at best. To that end, the Bundrant photo of John Wesley Hardin's brother was compared to a known photo of Jeff Hardin. The features matched.

To be sure, there was the process of eliminating the other brothers. A fairly easy task as Joseph, the oldest, was married when Mary was a teen, plus he was lynched in 1874. Brother Benjamin died at age nine. The youngest brother, James Gibson Barnett Hardin, was ruled out as he was not born until 1874. Therefore, Jeff, who was about fifteen or sixteen at the time, is the only brother of John Wesley to quality as the boyfriend of Mary Bundrant.[4]

Burndrant Sisters boyfriends. The one on the right just happened to be Jefferson Davis Hardin based on process of elimination. *Norman Wayne Brown collection.*

John Wesley Hardin was captured and sent to Texas state prison at Huntsville in 1878. It is almost ten years later that Jeff shows up again, now in the northeastern corner of the Texas Panhandle. The first documentation comes from Lipscomb County, Texas, a record of Jeff Hardin's marriage to Ida Mae Croussore on October 24, 1887.[5] Ida Mae was born May 6, 1872, in Kokomo, Indiana, to William Croussore and Nancy Browning.[6] No one seems to know why or how she landed in Texas.

By 1889, they were located in Mobeetie, Wheeler County, Texas. Their first child, John Wesley Hardin was born in February 1889 and his death certificate listed his place of birth as Mobeetie, Texas. Lipscomb and Wheeler counties are located in the northeastern corner of the Texas Panhandle.

This photograph from the Burndrant album enhanced and was featured on the cover of *Wild West History Association Journal*, August 2011. *Norman Wayne Brown collection.*

Walsenburg, located in Huerfano County, Colorado, was in the heart of a coal mining district and the population soared to around 20,000 at one time. Bob Ford, who assassinated the outlaw Jesse James, went to Walsenburg and ran a saloon and gambling house before moving on to Creede, Colorado. Jeff Hardin also showed up and opened a saloon as well. He and Ida's daughter, Mattie Belle, were born there on February 9, 1891.

Surprisingly, Ford liked to hang out at Hardin's saloon and was believed to be a great admirer of Jeff's brother, John Wesley. They were drinking together one night and got into an argument which led to gunplay. Both men drew their pistols and started shooting at each other at close range. A unique feature of the gunplay was both men used their free hand to slap at each other's gun

hand to spoil their aim. That resulted in wild shots going in all
directions. Consequently, both
stayed on their feet until all the
chambers of their six-guns were
spent. When the smoke cleared,
it was found, Hardin had been
shot in the shoulder and hand
while Ford was shot in a foot.
The end result of their antics
was both men were arrested
and jailed. They were released
with a fine and told that the
grass was a bit greener on up
the trail. Both heeded the advice as Bob Ford sold out and
headed for Creede, Colorado,
while Jeff Hardin sold out and
loaded his family in a covered
wagon and headed east for Indian Territory.[7]

Jeff Hardin's first cousin, Benjamin Columbus Hardin, Kent County survey-
or. His daughter Gussie married John
Snowden. *Courtesy Don Jay.*

Hardin decided his next
home and saloon would be in
Duncan, Indian Territory. Daughter, Della Lillian Hardin, was
born there on Dec. 14, 1893. While Jeff Hardin had changed locations, he did not change his ways. He continued to operate a
saloon, drink hard, gamble, and attract the drudges of society. Often times, his wife was in fear of her life due to the rowdy crowd
hanging around her husband. She would take the three children
and hide in a cornfield until the crowd left or passed out drunk.
In due course she decided she'd had enough and so she divorced
Hardin and moved back to Colorado.

She would not talk about the years of marriage to Hardin until
much later in life. Descendants claim Jeff Hardin killed a lawman
in Duncan and Ida feared for her children's safety. This could not
be substantiated. But something happened to make Ida Mae hide
from the notoriety of the Hardin name, for she changed her's and
the children's name to Davis. The name Davis remained forever-

Wedding photograph of Gussie Hardin and John Snowden. Couples married in Kent County were awarded a free lot in the now ghost town of Clairemont. *Courtesy Don Jay.*

more.[8]

After Ida Mae divorced Jeff, she and the children returned to Colorado and he went back to Junction, Texas. When John Wesley was released from prison on February 17, 1894, he first returned to Gonzales County. He received a full pardon on March 16, 1894, and by July 21, 1894, he was licensed to practice law.[9] He joined Jeff briefly before moving to El Paso in Early 1895.

Jeff moved from Junction to San Marcos, Hays County, Texas, about the same time his brother John moved to El Paso. He gained employment with the Hudson brothers, working at an artisan well. It didn't take Jeff long to stir up trouble. According to the *Houston Daily News* of April 9, 1895, Jeff Hardin was jailed and later released after he got into an argument with another employee named Ike Schroder. The argument escalated into a scuffle and Jeff stabbed the man with a knife. Someone patched Schroder up and took him home. There was no further mention of Schroder's condition, but he likely lived.[10]

Shortly thereafter, Hardin went back to Junction and on December 26, 1896, he married Mary Jane Taylor, daughter of the famous feudist Creed and Lavinia Amanda Spencer Taylor.[11] It is probable Jeff and Mary remained in the Junction area until about 1899. This is based primarily on a news report dated April 19, 1899, which reads, "Jeff Hardin was awarded $900 damages against the San Antonio and Arkansas Pass Railroad for personal injuries. Little else is known."

With $900 in his pocket, he probably thought it a good time to move away from his feuding in-laws (Taylor-Sutton faction). At any rate, Jeff and Mary moved to Kent County, Texas, in 1899.

John Snowden's father and brothers standing on the front of their porch at their ranch. *Courtesy Don Jay.*

Jeff's uncle, Benjamin Columbus Hardin, had previously settled his family there.

Upon arrival in Kent County, Hardin started raising horses. He owned the livery stable in Clairemont, was the constable there for a while, and a range detective for the Circle Bars Ranch. He rode with Pink Higgins, a well noted range detective and gunman, and John Snowden, another range detective and second cousin to Jeff by marriage. When citizens were allowed to file on state school land, Hardin filed on four sections, as allowed by law, but his claim was denied, as he had waited too long and did not meet the deadline.[12]

In early May 1901, Jeff Hardin's life changed. The catalytic agent about to amend his circumstances was John L. Stephenson, a horse trader out of Abilene. One fateful day he rode west and made a stop at Stokes stable in Colorado City. It was early May 1901. He stayed there for a few days and sold a couple of "jacks" before heading north to Snyder, a small town that started out as Snyder's Store. Stephenson then headed due north toward Kent County. He stopped to water his animals and make camp about thirteen miles north of Snyder, at Ennis Creek Bridge, just inside

Scurry County.

At the same time riding south from Clairemont, Kent County, was Jeff Hardin and John L. Snowden. They were driving a herd of horses to water at the creek and looking for a rustler believed to be working in the area. Late in the day they approached Ennis Creek and spotted Stephenson. Hardin told Snowden the man fit the description of the rustler they were looking for. Hardin confronted the man. Stephenson and Hardin argued.

The details are unknown but there were two possibilities. One is that Jeff believed he was the rustler and threw down on him without giving the man a chance. The other, and most logical reason for the argument was over the water at the creek. Ranchers often used a fort scraper to dig depressions in dry creek beds. One can dig down less than a foot in those dry creek beds and water will fill the pockets.

Hardin probably had what he considered his own private watering hole and resented the horse trader watering his stock at his spot. Regardless, Hardin drew his .45 caliber revolver and shot the man in the face, below the right eye. When they approached him, Stephenson was still breathing so they mounted up and rode to a ranch about three miles away and borrowed a wagon and team and returned to the scene. They placed the mortally wounded man in the bed of the wagon and drove him the thirteen miles to Snyder, being it was the nearest town with a doctor. Mr. Stephenson died the next day while at the home of the doctor.[13]

The sheriff of Scurry County questioned both Hardin and Snowden and told Hardin there would be an inquest to determine if he would be officially charged with murder. This did not set well with Jeff Hardin because his partner, John Snowden, refused to go along with him and say the victim was armed. This created a problem for Jeff, as Snowden refused to lie for him. He and Snowden returned to Kent County to await the inquest that never came.[14]

At some point in time, Hardin had turned a small room of his livery stable into a saloon. It was a small, rough place, not only in clientele but aesthetically as well, having a bar, one table and chairs on a dirt floor. On Tuesday night, October 8, 1901, (some say it was on a Saturday night) Jeff confronted Snowden in the saloon, over his lack of support in the Scurry County incident, telling him that a relative should try to help his kin. Snowden did not see any obligation and continued his refusal to lie for Jeff. They argued and things got so heated everyone left the saloon. Then Jeff called Snowden back into the saloon. There were no known eye-witnesses to the three shots heard as the clock struck 10 p.m.

Snowden ran out the door and fled to the house of his father-in-law, that being Ben Hardin. He said, "I've shot Jeff Hardin and I think I killed him."

Ben told Snowden that he had better leave the country or the law would hang him for sure. He made a horse available to him, but Snowden went to the constable and turned himself in. The sheriff and constable went to the scene of the killing and found Jeff Hardin lying on the floor. His revolver was on the floor behind the bar, so he may have had time to draw, or the pistol slipped out of his holster when he fell. Another possibility was that Snowden removed his pistol from the holster after he killed him, but that was unlikely, as the pistol was on the floor behind the bar. One bullet entered Hardin's heart and exited below the shoulder blade. One bullet shattered the left leg, and the third shot hit Hardin in the right leg. Hardin's weapon was not fired, and Snowden was uninjured. Apparently the first shot hit Hardin in the heart, killing him instantly and as he fell, Snowden fired twice more, hitting him in the legs.[15]

It is unknown if Snowden left the country following the gunfight. Descendants say he did. The talk was that Snowden had to murder him because no one could stand up to Jeff Hardin in a fair fight and live to tell it. Regardless of the veracity of this rumor, Snowden was charged with murder and released on $5,000 bond—but never tried. It is not known why, for documentation on the Stephenson murder is not on file in Scurry County; including indication of any inquest being scheduled on Jeff Hardin. It is likely the paperwork was disposed of by the District Attorney after the death of Hardin.

Stephenson was a widower, and his children became wards of Taylor County, over in Abilene. His name was printed in the newspaper erroneously as J. L. Stevenson, who was a politician, also from Abilene. No living politician likes it when they read in

Jeff Hardin's stable in Clairemont. He turned the tack room (far right of building) into a saloon with dirt floor and one table. Later, the stable was owned by C. O. Fox. His wife was Fannie Hardin Fox, second cousin to Jeff and John Wesley Hardin. *Courtesy Don Jay.*

the paper that they were killed as a suspected cattle thief and add insult to injury by receiving cards and letters of condolence from friends and supporters. Like a true politician he said, "This manifestation of friendship is very gratifying to me, but I would like to have it understood that my anatomy has not been punctured by a bullet. It was a Mr. Stevenson who suffered the misfortune." But then, that's another story.[16]

John Snowden, his wife Gussie, her sister, Fannie Hardin Fox, and her husband, Charlie Fox, packed up in covered wagons in 1903 and moved to Cripple Creek, Colorado, where they went into the gold mining business. Gussie and the children died in the flu epidemic of 1918 in Teller County, Colorado, and John was still there in 1920. No record of his death has been found but Snowden never returned to Texas. His in-laws, the Fox family, returned after about a year and went back to ranching on the 24 Ranch in Kent County.

Ida Mae Croussore Hardin Davis remarried Mansford Inskeep on January 29, 1896, in La Junta, Colorado. They had three children together before Ida divorced him. She then married a third

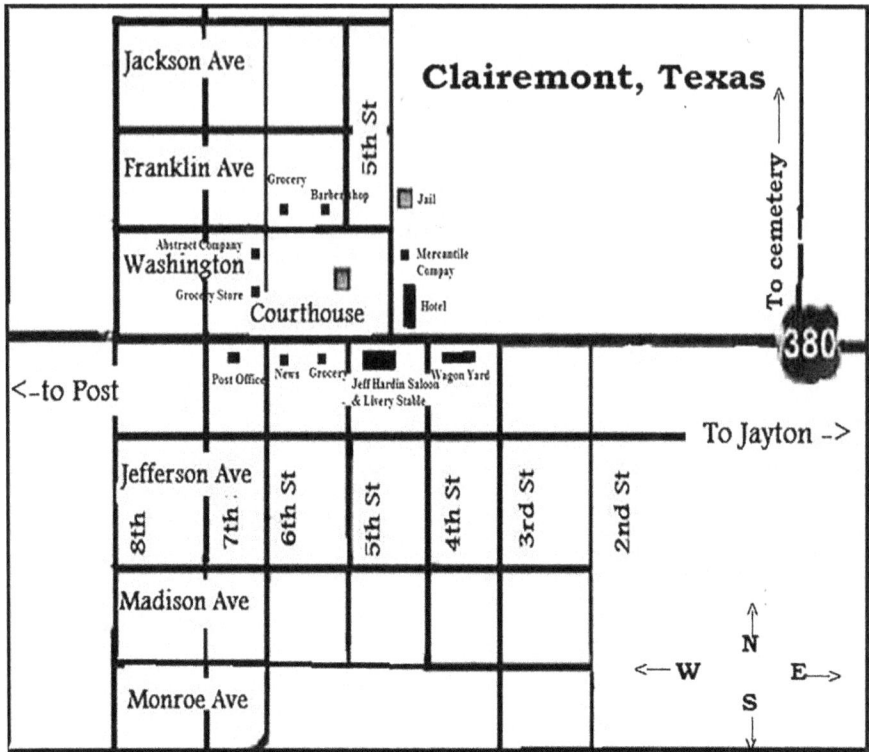

Map of Clairemont showing the known locations of some businesses in the township.
Map design by Norman Wayne Brown.

time to John Fanning. She died in Green County, Missouri, on
June 10, 1946. Ida Mae never returned to Texas. Jeff's wife, Mary,
remarried a man named Blount and they moved to Arizona. Mary
never returned to Texas.

Jeff Hardin was buried in the city cemetery at Clairemont, and
his headstone does not give the date of his death, only the year of
nineteen and aught one.

A note inside a bottle was found at the base of Hardin's
gravesite by a Hardin descendant some years ago. It had been
written and left by Cleve Hardin, a son of Jeff and Mary. It said: "I
am in my 80s now and I have been coming here every summer for
my entire adult life. But, I am getting old and unable to travel, so
this is my last farewell, Dad."[17]

Chapter Ten
Gunfight in Jeff D. Hardin's Saloon
By Norman Wayne Brown

This story was published in the Journal of Wild West History Association, June, 2014 issue. *Reprinted with permission.*

When I first wrote about Jeff Hardin, younger brother of the notorious gunfighter John Wesley Hardin, errors were made which needed correcting. Like all stories, we often make new discoveries from the other side of the fence after stories have been put into print. In this case, it was a couple of newspaper reports and a taped interview about John L. Snowden, the man who killed Jeff Hardin.[1]

Charlie Snowden, brother of John L. Snowden, said, "Jeff Hardin wanted to be like his brother Wes, a big bad gunfighter."[2] Jeff had his first reported gunfight with Robert Ford, the murderer of Jesse James. Both men received minor injuries after expending all the bullets from their revolvers and were run out of town.[3]

Later, down in Bastrop, Texas, Jeff got into an affray with a saddle shop owner and that

Jefferson Davis Hardin wearing his six-gun, circa 1900. *Courtesy grandson, Jeff D. Hardin.*

gunfight ended with, a bullet to Jeff's chest, nicking his right lung. He was treated and recovered in Junction, Texas, under the care of his brother Gip.[4]

Later Jeff got into an argument with a co-worker, Ike Schroder, in San Marcos, and stabbed him. It is unknown if the man recovered or died from the injury. Then, Jeff got into a poker game in Fort Worth, and pulled a "Wes Hardin" by trying to take the pot from the table. It backfired and he was arrested, then released on bond.

He boarded the train for Colorado, (renamed Colorado City in 1907) Texas, and the conductor took possession of his weapons. It was a rule that no guns were allowed in the passenger cars. A group of men jumped Jeff and assaulted him, then left the train. So far, there were no reported killings by Jeff Hardin.

The story was from the *Colorado Clipper* in Colorado City and printed again by *Coming West*, Snyder, Texas, dated March 21, 1901:

> When the passenger pulled in this morning from the east, Jeff Hardin, who lives in Kent County, and who had previously had some trouble at Ft. Worth, for which he was under bond, stepped off the train with his Winchester in hand and related to Sheriff Delling and others a very lenghty [sic] experience he had on the train that pulled out of Ft. Worth last night. He says that before he was aware of it several men crowded him and punched him around after the conductor had taken his gun. As soon as the gang that assailed him had finished their work they got off the train and were seen no more. Mr. Hardin wears a bruise about the left ear and is black about the right eye. He is very sore from his treatment and necessarily angered because the cowards who clubbed in on him could not be found in time for a settlement. It is said that Hardin is game and about the only way those toughs could handle him was to have caught him unaware and in over powering numbers.

Back in Clairemont, up in Kent County, Jeff bought a livery stable. He turned the tack room into a little saloon. It had a dirt floor, one table, and four chairs, along with a crude bar counter.

Jeff also owned horses and worked as a "scalper" for local ranchers. A scalper was what Hollywood called a range detective. Each time a scalper apprehended a cattle thief, he was paid a fee by the appropriate rancher.[5]

Jeff married Mary Taylor, youngest daughter of the famous Creed Taylor, down in Junction, prior to moving to Kent County. Jeff and Wes Hardin were first cousins to Benjamin Columbus Hardin, a well-respected surveyor of Kent County. John Love Snowden married one of Ben's daughters,

Standing: Will Snowden and Bill Neely. Seated: Will Rogers and John L. Snowden. John Snowden seated far right. *Courtesy Don Jay.*

Augustus "Gussie" Hardin. That made John and Gussie Snowden second cousins to Jeff Hardin. Snowden, a quite reserved man, was a cowboy and scalper and sometimes rode with Jeff.[6]

On the 5th day of May 1901, Jeff told Snowden he was going to ride down to Snyder and asked if he wanted to go. Snowden agreed and they saddled up and headed south. When they approached Ennis Creek, just inside Scurry County, they saw a man mounted on horseback. When they rode up to him, Jeff pulled his pistol and told the man that he thought he was a cattle thief.

There were no cows anywhere to be seen. An argument ensued and Jeff shot the man in the face. The .45 caliber bullet entered below eye level and exited behind his head, above an ear. Family lore indicated the man was taken to the doctor in Snyder and died the next day. Actually, the man John L. Stevenson, a bona fide horse trader out of Abilene, was treated by Doctor Leslie and

A rare photograph of the Clairemont Hotel located east, across from the courthouse. Judge Cullen Higgins was killed in this hotel by Si Bostick. *Courtesy Scurry County Museum, Snyder, Texas.*

did not die as previously reported. He wrote a letter to the editor about a month after the injury, thanking the good doctor for the fine treatment he had received under his care.[7]

Mr. J. L. Stevenson's letter was printed in the Snyder, Texas, newspaper, *Coming West,* as follows:

May 17, 1901: Abilene, Texas,

During my recent stay in Snyder when severely wounded, the people extended to me and my daughter many kindnesses and courteses [sic].

We were strangers to the whole people, and are yet strangers to many persons who showed us great favors, and it would be impossible for us to personally acknowledge our indeptedness [sic] to each one who so kindly ministered to us in time of need.

We, therefore, adopt this method of extending to each and every one our sincere and heartfelt thanks for their attention to us, in the trying ordeal through which we passed.

Without intending to draw comparisons, for that would be well-nigh impossible, we desire to specially extend our thanks to Mr. Beck, justice of the peace, and

to Dr. Leslie, for their untiring efforts to make me com-
fortable. Again, we thank the city of Snyder, one and
all.

On the way home to Clairemont, Jeff told Snowden he wanted
him to swear that Stevenson drew a gun on him, knowing the man
was unarmed. Snowden refused, saying he would lie for no man.
Jeff told him, "If you don't, I just might shoot you too. I aim to
collect my fifty dollars for him."

Snowden knew that danger lay ahead concerning Jeff Hardin.
Jeff was in trouble and if convicted in court, could receive a prison
term for murder if the man died, or attempted murder if he survived.[8]

Jeff collected his fifty dollars from a rancher, claiming the victim was a cattle thief, when in fact, he was a horse trader out of
Abilene. He continually harassed John Snowden by threatening
him. John Snowden met with three Texas Rangers and told them
about the incident and his fear that Jeff would try to kill him.[9]

Late Tuesday afternoon, October 8, 1901, in Jeff's saloon, Jeff
told Snowden again, "If you don't say that man was heeled and

Doctor A. C. Leslie, *circa* 1901. He treated a gunshot victim and nursed him back to
health after being shot in the face by Jeff Hardin. *Courtesy Scurry County Museum, Snyder,
Texas.*

Jeff D. Hardin's grave in the Clairemont Cemetery. The grave was in a bad state of repair when this author took the photo some years ago. The cedar flies were swarming that day. A pill bottle was found in the crack to the right. It contained a farewell note written by Cleve, a son of Jeff. It was his last trip to Clairemont from Arizona. *Photograph taken by Norman Wayne Brown.*

drawing down on me, I'm going to kill you."

They argued and Snowden left and went home around sundown. Later that evening, someone came to Snowden's place and told him that Jeff Hardin wanted him to come to the saloon, that he wanted to talk to him. Snowden knew this was probably a set-up, so he strapped on his six-gun and grabbed a lantern and headed for the saloon. As he entered the little dirt floor establishment it was completely dark inside. Snowden raised the lantern in time to see Jeff pointing a pistol at him and then Jeff fired one shot. It missed him. Snowden quickly drew his pistol and fired three times and Jeff went down as his pistol fell from his hand. One shot was to the heart and one to each leg. He was probably dead when he hit the floor.[10]

That night, Mary Taylor Hardin, became a widow with two young sons and was pregnant with another child. After she buried her husband, Jeff, in the Clairemont cemetery, she rented the livery stable to a local citizen and sold off the stock. She kept the animals needed to pull her wagonload of goods and her small children.

She went home to her father's place near Junction.

There, her third son was born. Later, she remarried Robert Blount and they returned to Clairemont where Robert operated the livery stable for a couple of years and then he and Mary sold out to C. O. Fox. They moved back to the Junction area where an intriguing story took place. The Blount couple and the Hardin sons went by wagon train to Arizona where they remained until Mary and Robert divorced. Robert then returned to Texas and remained.[9]

In later years, Mary told her grandson, Jeff Hardin, that her husband, Jeff Hardin, did not have a gun with him the night he was killed. She stated that he left it in the livery stable. Also, it was reported that a man by the name of Underwood was a witness to the gunfight but was afraid to come forth. Did Jeff really fire first? Was he even armed? Why was Underwood afraid? Did John Snowden tell the truth to his brother Charlie who submitted to a taped interview that Jeff was out to kill him and fired first? According to a news report there was a pistol found on the floor after the gunfight.

Some events from the past will forever remain sketchy and foggy and all we know for sure is, Jefferson Davis Hardin, younger brother of John Wesley Hardin, finally mimicked him completely; both killed in gunfights, both killed in a saloon in West Texas, and both just a little late on the shoot.

Chapter Eleven
Belle Of the Plains, Arabella Adams Hardin

By Norman Wayne Brown

This story was published by *The Tombstone Epitaph*, August, 2021 issue. *Reprinted with permission.*

In the year 1850, Samuel H. and Sarah P. Hill Adams entered their eighth child's name in the family *Bible*. Even so, she did not like the name they gave her. Apparently, Arabella just didn't fit as far as she was concerned. She liked Allie Belle, or Alie, or just Belle better. Her father-in-law would refer to her as just Bell.

She would grow up to marry Joseph Gibson Hardin, the oldest son of Reverend James Gibson and Mary Elizabeth Dixon Hardin. Joseph usually went by Joe or J. G. and was the older brother of the notorious gunfighter, John Wesley Hardin. Had his parents known of the violence that was to come to him and his brothers in later years, it would have pained their hearts like fires from Hell. But those were difficult times and Texas was a wild frontier with little or no law to speak of.

Joseph Gibson Hardin would marry Arabella Adams on September 22, 1871, in Cherokee, Texas, about seventy miles south of Joe's home in Comanche.[1] She listed her first name as Bell for the marriage record. While she was listed as three years of age on the 1850 census, her death certificate recorded her birth date of August 31, 1850. The census taker should have written three months of age, not three years. Cherokee is an unincorporated community in San Saba County, in western Central Texas.[2]

Being Arabella evidently didn't like her first name, she went by Allie Belle and at other times just Belle. She signed her name with one L, "Alie," and her signature was on many land transactions as a witness for husband Joe Hardin. Joe accumulated vast land holdings by fraud and his worth in 1874 was around

$25,000, with thousands of acres of land. Joe became a shyster, a wheeler dealer, who sold cattle he did not have and after selling them he then went out and bought them. Today, he would have been classified as a "white collar criminal."

The Adams family came out of Tennessee to Honey Grove, Washington County, Texas, between 1854-1859. In 1860, the Adams family was living in Fannin County, Texas, where Arabella's father was a sixty-year-old blacksmith. She was

Joe and Arabella Adams Hardin. Possibly a wedding photograph. *Chuck Parsons collection.*

listed in the census as Arabel snd was listed as age eleven.

On or before 1870 her father, Samuel Adams, died. Then, in the 1870 census, Arabella's mother, Sallie Adams, is listed as widowed and listed as S. P., age sixty-one, living near Fort Worth, Tarrant County, Texas. Arabella is listed as eighteen-year-old Rabella. It is unclear why or when Arabella Adams appeared in Cherokee to meet and marry Joseph Hardin.

Joseph Gibson Hardin and his cousins, Tom and Bud Dixon, were lynched on May 31, 1874, in Comanche, when a hostile mob lynched them after Joe's brother, John Wesley, had allegedly killed Deputy Sheriff Charles Webb in Comanche.

After Joe was hanged, Belle managed to contact her family in Mount Calm and a relative went to Comanche and took her and the little ones back with him. She was only able to save a few personal items of Joe's such as his desk nameplate, his bank book, a permit to practice law, a certificate of his appointment as Comanche County Treasurer, and a commission of his appointment as a postmaster in Comanche in 1872.

Belle lived alone raising their two children, Joseph Jr. and

Joseph Gibson Hardin when he was younger. The photo, which we know is authentic as it was in Hardin's personal tintype album with other images of his family. *Chuck Parsons collection.*

Dora. She received a letter from Joe's father, Reverend James Gibson Hardin, dated November 10, 1875, and posted from Dodd City, Texas. Most interesting is the fact that Joe's parents still considered Belle part of the family and gave directions to their home. The Reverend died the following year and while his burial site is unknown, it is very likely he was buried near his home in Red River County. The letter is transcribed as follows:

Dear Bell--------
I am here, just starting home for Red River County. I have been attending Court at Bonham. One of my mules died with the blind staggers while here. We are always glad to hear from you and the sweet little ones. God bless you and them. My address is Paris, Lamar County. We have a good home but hard run. We live twenty miles from Paris, near Dinwitty,s [Dinwiddie] saw mill 10 miles north of Starkville.[Now Detroit] We would be glad [if] you could come and spend two or three months with us or as long as you could. The cars [train] run in nine miles of Paris to Brookston. You could [get] there on the cars and get a hack to drive you out. All want to see you. Write soon-My love to both Bent [Benton] Cobb and wife [daughter Elizabeth] and Effie. Excuse this hurried letter. My brother Robert from Brenham was up to see me yesterday and Jeff and Nannie are here with me. Sweet peace to you.
　　　　　Your Loving Father-in-law James Hardin.

Reverend Hardin was correct when he wrote that his home was twenty miles from Paris. He traveled ten miles east to Starkville and ten miles due north almost to the town of Woodland. The post office at Starkville was moved a short distant to Bennett Station when the railroad came. Later the station was renamed Detroit.[3] No records have been uncovered to indicate Belle took her father-in-law up on the visit. Reverend Hardin's reference to Bent Cobb, wife, and Effie was meant for his daughter, Elizabeth "Lizzie" Hardin, who married Joseph Benton Cobb in Comanche County on November 8, 1872.

What led to the tragedy in Comanche on May 26, 1874?

Joe Hardin pulled a gun on Henry Ware and Henry ran to the Sheriff's office to lodge a complaint. This led to Brown County Deputy Sheriff Charles Webb's run-in with John Wesley Hardin and associates. Deputy Webb was killed in the affray which led to Wes Hardin's parents, brother Joe and cousins, Bud and Tom Dixon, being taken into protective custody.

It is odd that shackles were put around the necks of Joe Hardin and his Dixon cousins. Joe and his two cousins were taken from protective custody by an unknown mob and hanged. Joe deserved a fair trial for his crimes, but no jury would have given him the death sentence for being a shyster. The hanging of the Dixon boys was also unjustified as there were no warrants out for their arrest. Some reports lay claim that Texas Rangers were behind the hangings. Based on Texas Ranger Captain Waller's demeanor as a brutal man, anything is possible.[4]

Belle had little Joe and Dora to raise after Joseph was hanged. Somehow, she got by, possibly on funds left from her husband Joe's business. Some years later she met Joseph Wood Pierce, said to be a Mississippi gambler.[5] They were married December 10, 1879, in Groesbeck, Limestone County, Texas, and per 1880 census were living in Mt. Calm, Limestone County. They were recorded as J. W. Pierce and Alla Bell Hardin. Her son, Joseph, and daughter, Dora, were living with her and Mr. Pierce. He had two children from a previous marriage, son, Charles, age thirteen and daughter, Stella, age eight.

Ironically, Mr. Pierce married his first wife Margaret V. Thermon, November 2, 1854, in Cherokee, Texas, the same place where Allie Belle married Joseph Hardin. She and Mr. Pierce had a

Cherokee, Texas where Joe and Arabella were married. *Norman Wayne Brown collection.*

daughter born in September 1883 named Anna Lee Pierce.

By 1900, Belle is located in Concho County, Texas, as widow Allie B. Pierce. She was a stock raiser and had daughter, Anna Lee Pierce, age seventeen, living with her. She had a female boarder in the house, a twenty-nine-year-old music teacher named Stubblefield. Her son, Joseph G., and his wife, Ada, and children were living in the house next to her and he was working for her as a stock herder.

Then, on January 7, 1906, her daughter, Anna Lee [Lea], married James Arthur Edmiston at Concho County. By 1910, Belle is listed as widow Bell Pierce and living with son, Joe, and his wife, Ada, in Ballinger, Runnells County, Texas, where Joe was running a wood and coal yard. In the 1920 census, the Joe Hardin family was still in Ballinger and Joe was working as an agent for Gulf Roofing. Belle had moved to San Angelo and living with her daughter, Anne Lee Edminston, and her husband who was a farmer. Anna Lee became a clothing saleslady in San Angelo and died there on March 9, 1964. The informant on her death certificate listed her mother as Allie Belle Callihan in error and her father as Wood Pierce.

Sometime after 1920, Belle moved to Coleman, Texas, to live with her daughter, Dora Henderson, and her husband. She fell and fractured a hip which led to her death on May 24, 1929. Her daughter, Dora, was the informant, and she was listed as Allie Belle Pierce. She was almost seventy-nine-years-old. Her date of birth was August 31, 1850. She was buried the next day in the Paint Rock Cemetery, Concho County, Texas. Her stepdaughter, Stella W. Pierce Hargis, is buried near her. Ironically, her son, Joseph Gibson Hardin Jr., died June 22, 1929, only twenty-nine days after her death.

Arabella Adams! Allie Belle Hardin! Belle Hardin! Allie Belle Pierce! Belle Pierce! A. B. Pierce! A beautiful woman! Belle came a long way from her birthplace in Sumner County, Tennessee, daughter of a blacksmith, to live

The engraving was labeled John Wesley Hardin, printed in Hardin's autobiography and which later the publishers said was actually Joe Hardin, not John. That was their error. *Chuck Parsons collection.*

and experience events that most of us could only dream about or have nightmares about. She was married to a wealthy, but crooked man, adored his parents and probably loathed her brother-in-law, the gun fighting Wes Hardin.

She went from a crooked husband to wed again to a gambling man. After he died, she surfaced as a successful cattle rancher, outliving two husbands and raising four children. But her heart was not in Tennessee, her birthplace, nor Comanche, Texas, where so much violence took place and where her man was lynched by a mob. Her heart seemed to be in a place where she found peace, that being among the memories of her family near Paint Rock, a beautiful place where she was laid to rest. Had Belle been written about years ago, she would likely have been pegged as the "Belle of the Plains." Could it be that after all this time, she still is that Belle of the Plains?

Chapter Twelve
Kent County Hardin Kin

By Norman Wayne Brown

This story has not previously been published.

In a book, *The History of Kent County, Texas*, it was stated: "John Wesley Hardin visited his cousins in Kent County often." That proved to be a problem. There was Benjamin Columbus Hardin, a first cousin, and Jeff D. Hardin, John Wesley's little brother. There were many second cousins like Mark "Uncle Buck" Hardin, Ben's four beautiful daughters, Fannie, Gussie, Martha, and Bertha. All of these cousins arrived in Kent County after John Wesley's death at El Paso, in 1895.

Most of the cousins arrived in 1898 from various locations throughout Texas. First cousin, Ben Hardin, went to Kent County to try and rid himself of hired killers out to do him harm. All of the cousins knew or knew of the notorious gunfighter cousin, but only his brother, Jeff Hardin, had any respect for him.[1]

The committee who put the history together admitted being biased to a degree as they decided nothing negative would be printed. Therefore, the gunfight between Jeff Hardin and John Snowden was omitted. The killing of nine men over the theft of one black cow was ignored. The murder of Judge Cullen Higgins by Si Bostick went by the wayside as well.

While the population of Kent County was low, the killings were high. The colorful life and times of Guff Lafoon also went by the wayside. Lafoon was a snake showman, a cowboy, range cook, and junkyard magnate. He had the largest used parts store in West Texas. He hid his money inside the cylinders of old vehicle engines, but could not remember which junk vehicles contained his stash of silver dollars. So, when he made a contract with the government to buy them during World War II, he required them

Fannie Hardin Fox standing in the back of a wagon by the Kent County Courthouse, holding her baby girl who died at age eight. Note the man upper right on the balcony of Clairemont Hotel. *Courtesy Don Jay.*

Kent County Jail after being remodeled. The older jail had sheriff quarters upstairs. When he moved the county removed the upper level. Only one man ever escaped but was captured later that day hiding on the roof of the courthouse. *Norman Wayne Brown collection.*

to remove the heads from all engines so he could reclaim the coinage. When he took the sack of coins to the bank the count caused him to faint. He was worth a fortune but had no electricity or running water in his house. He rode his horse to the Cowboy Reunion at Stamford well into his seventies.

Clairemont was a small West Texas cow town when Kent County was organized in 1892. The county of about 300 people doubled in size within a few years. One of the newcomers, not related to the Hardins, was Pink Higgins who

The four daughters of Benjamin C. Hardin. Seated left to right: Fannie and Gussie. Standing left to right: Martha and Bertha. *Courtesy Don Jay.*

came to Kent County in 1899 from Lampasas County and started a cattle ranch.

Trouble soon brewed when Higgins met a neighbor, J. William "Billy" Standifer. The two range riders differed as the result of an old grievance and Higgins shot and killed Standifer on October 1, 1902. Pink told Sheriff B. F. Roy that he thought he had killed Standifer. The Sheriff's reply to Higgins was, "If I wasn't sure, I had better go back and finish."

Stories like those are part of Kent County's history.

One Hardin cousin, Fannie Hardin Fox, took her grandson, Don Jay, to a picture show in 1954 to see a movie titled *The Lawless Breed*, staring Rock Hudson. After the movie little Don said to his grandmother, "Grandma, weren't we related to that John Wesley Hardin?"

"Heaven's no," she replied. "He was just trash." That statement led these authors to title our biography on Hardin as *A Law-*

Typical homestead box and strip home. Most homes were dugouts until around 1910. Left to right Gussie Hardin Snowden, her sister Martha, Charlie Addie and little girl on the horse. *Courtesy Don Jay.*

Fannie Hardin Fox was second cousin to John Wesley Hardin but would not claim it. She refused to ride sidesaddle. *Norman Wayne Brown collection.*

Mark "Uncle Buck" Hardin, older brother of Martin Quilla Hardin. He was the county clerk of Kent and a minister. He carried a satchel that contain a *Bible* and a six-gun. *Norman Wayne Brown collection.*

less Breed . . .[2]

When Don Jay was in college at Texas Tech in Lubbock, he penned a number of magazine articles about the Hardin clan. One, written in 1967 was titled *Bad Blood* and covered the gunfight of Jeff Hardin. It was based mostly on family lore, with many inaccuracies. However, he did get it right that all four Hardin brothers died violently. Of course, no one knew at the time about the cause of death for Gip Hardin.

Jeff Hardin owned and operated a stable in Clairemont, and kept a ledger. That ledger was passed down to his grandson, Jeff D. Hardin of Arizona. Jeff sent this author a copy of the ledger shortly before he died. Interesting was the fact that Jeff had a number of Hardin relatives in the county who stabled their horses with him.

From the ledger was Mark Hardin, county clerk and rancher. He was known as "Uncle Buck." He was also a minister and carried a satchel that a cowboy once discovered , held a *Bible* and a six-gun. Uncle Buck was very outspoken and didn't like anyone disagreeing with his point of view. He once took a trip to visit family back in Tennessee and a steamboat captain doubted his word and he quickly threw the captain overboard.[3]

Don Jay had a large photo album and did not know anything about one man's photo that said on the backside, "Uncle Buck." It was Mark Hardin.

Others in the ledger included Benjamin Columbus "Ben" Hardin, county surveyor. He lost an arm in an ambush but never found out who or why he was shot. Rube Hardin, was the son of Mark. John Snowden, cousin by marriage to Jeff Hardin and was the man who killed Jeff in a gunfight in Jeff's saloon. Fannie Har-

Jim Miller and friend. Frequently identified as John Wesley Hardin, the man is most likely Martin Q. Hardin, a cousin of infamous John Wesley Hardin. *Courtesy Bill C. James.*

din Fox was a second cousin.

Uncle Buck was a regular at camp meetings; especially the ones held by his friend, Uncle Kin Elkins, down in the southeast corner of the county, at Polar. Those camp meetings lasted for a minimum of a week every year. People came from miles around and stayed the entire week, sleeping on the ground and consuming meals prepared by chuck wagon cooks.

His brother, Martin Quilla Hardin, was friends with his cousin, John Wesley Hardin. Martin, better known as Mart, may have been a Texas Ranger at some point in time but it is documented that he was a farm laborer in Johnson County, Texas, in 1880.

Jim Miller and Martin Quilla Hardin had been in Pecos attempting to shoot down Sheriff Bud Frazer. Their trial was moved to El Paso and of course John Wesley, having a law degree, was the defense attorney for Miller. There is an image of Jim Miller and another man believed to be Martin Q. Hardin.

Later he moved to Lordsburg, New Mexico, to live out a very interesting life as a postmaster, deputy US marshal, and political leader. It is unlikely that he and brother Buck's paths ever crossed again after leaving Savannah, Tennessee.[4]

Fannie Hardin was in a photograph taken by the Kent County

Courthouse. She was standing in the wagon with her little girl who died at about age eight. In the image, to the right was a man sitting up on a platform. It was said that he was on the balcony of the Clairemont Hotel. But no image could be found of the hotel, only the courthouse, stable, and jail. Then, a photograph was found in the Scurry County Museum, Snyder, Texas, in a file of some family who had a family reunion there and had a photograph taken. It was on that balcony that the man appeared in the wagon by the courthouse photograph.

Martin "Mart" Quilla Hardin, brother to Uncle Buck Hardin of Kent County may have been the only Hardin to have a sense of humor. A newspaper reported that he said to a friend, "Well, we buried Santa Fe Charlie today."

"You mean he was dead?"

"Yes, that's why we buried him."

"He was young. What killed him?"

"Five aces."

Chapter Thirteen
Wagon Train To Arizona

By Norman Wayne Brown

This story was published in *The Tombstone Epitaph,* June 2018 issue. *Reprinted with permission.*

One born in Texas is referred to as a "Native Texan" and those who came to Texas by hook or crook, or running from the law were/are referred to as transplanted. It was a matter of choice. They say it grows on you and you'll never want to leave. If that's the case, it makes one wonder why a number of native-born Texans would just up and leave the land of milk and honey? Well, there was law in Texas as well.

Cleburn Hardin, nicknamed Cleve and sometimes Clebe, son of John Wesley Hardin's little brother, Jeff D., and Mary Taylor Hardin, penned an unpublished journal many years ago describing how his family shifted around in Texas from one place to another until they finally decided to leave by wagon train for that far western state of Arizona. While he gave a good account of the trip, he did not give any indication to why the family wanted to leave the nest and go west in 1917.

Cleve Hardin's name appears on a headstone in the Clairemont graveyard. But it was his father, Jeff D. Hardin, planted there. When, in later years the headstone was erected it gave Jeff's death of 1901 with no month or day. Like his brother John Wesley Hardin, Jeff was killed in a gunfight in his saloon in Clairemont on October 8, 1901, a little over six years after his notorious gunslinger brother died on the floor of a saloon in El Paso. His three sons' names were chiseled underneath his name but not Jeff's wife's name. She was the youngest daughter of Creed Taylor.

Mary Taylor Hardin went home to her parents each time she became pregnant, no matter where she and husband Jeff Hardin

Moses Waddle married one of Creed Taylor's daughters. He planted the seed that led to three of Creed Taylor daughters forming a wagon train to Arizona. *Norman Wayne Brown collection.*

were living. The home she went to was the Taylor Ranch in Kimble County, Texas near the town of Noxville.[1] A historical marker is displayed where the ranch house once stood.[2]

Creed Taylor gave each of his children 160 acres of land and Mary's land was four miles south of Creed's house. This is where she went when her husband, Jeff Hardin, was killed in a gunfight in 1901 up in Kent County.[3]

Mary remained at Noxville until she married Robert Koin Blount in 1907. They moved back to Kent County and Blount ran the livery stable for several years. After 1910 they moved to Eden, Texas. From there they moved west of Kerrville on the Guadalupe River. The kids went to school at Hunt, about twenty miles west of Kerrville.

When Mary's son, Cleve [Clebe], was fourteen (born in 1899), around 1913, they sold out and moved to Victoria where Bob Blount hauled cedar. Then they moved to Lomita, Texas, on the Colorado River. There Cleve and Buster attended school during the year of 1915. Cleve was then age sixteen.[4]

A couple of years later Mary Taylor Hardin Blount received a letter from her sister, Leta Minnie Taylor, who had married a man named Moses Waddle. Now, there's a truly biblical name; the man who led his people from years of wandering the wilderness . . . "Moses then led his people eastward, beginning the long journey to Canaan. The procession moved slowly and found it necessary to encamp three times."

Now, if the parents of Moses Waddle had any hopes of their son growing up and being a protégé of "the Moses," they were surely disappointed. Rather than being like the biblical Moses, he was more of a "worm." And maybe that's why young Moses Waddle went by Joe for his first name of Joseph. And he didn't even try to walk in the footsteps of the biblical Joseph, husband of

Mary. On the other hand, Waddle may have read some of Moses' exploits in the family *Bible*.

He did lead his people, a small group, out of Texas, which had not long graduated from being wilderness, westward to Arizona. However, when he left it was not that he was seeking an adventure but was running from the law. Waddle got into trouble over a yearling found in his possession and not wearing his brand. The report was he had stolen the yearling. A family member claimed he was framed by Giles Sumlin [Summerlin] of Thorndale, Texas, saying he was the one who stole the yearling.

Waddle's uncle and aunt, Tom and Mary Barber, told him he had better go somewhere and get away, as Giles Sumlin had money and power and knew he would be blamed and sent to the pen. Waddle had left his wife, Molly, and married Mary's sister, Leta Minnie Gertrude Taylor, then fleeing to Arizona. They had two sons, Grover and Lee. He failed to mention to anyone that he had left his first wife Molly in Thorndale.[5]

He brought his wife and sneaked back into Texas in 1917. He, maybe with the help of Leta, talked the Blounts into going back to Arizona with them. They agreed and loaded up everything in three wagons and Cleve Hardin wrote that his uncle, Moses "Joe" Waddle, loaded up his family in two wagons and the train headed west.[6]

"We had about twenty head of horses and mules," Cleve explained. "I drove the water wagon and my mother, Mary, took all of the furniture she owned, and it fit in one wagon. While she was proud of her possessions, I believe all of it could have been replaced for not more than $100."

She took her chickens on the trip and would turn them loose when they stopped to camp and put them back in the coop come dark. After passing through Fort Stockton, they entered the vast and empty prairieland between there and El Paso.

"There was not one stick of wood on that prairie and there were no longer any buffalo chips to burn," Cleve reported.

They were thankful to the West Texas cattlemen as "cow chips" were in abundance.[7]

They finally made El Paso and continued westward and entered New Mexico. When they arrived at Deming, they had traveled around 600 miles from Hunt, Texas. They stopped in Deming, New Mexico, to rest the horses as well as themselves. World War I broke out when they arrived. They decided to find work and replenish the purse. They stayed only a month, hitched up and traveled on.

Sometime later they entered Arizona and stopped at Temple around the first day of September 1917. They needed money and all obtained field jobs picking cotton. Cleve was called up by the draft, but the war ended the day he was supposed to sign-up.[8]

Mary Taylor Hardin Blount and her sons years later in Arizona where they stayed. Mary divorced Mr. Blount and he returned to Texas. *Courtesy grandson, Jeff D. Hardin.*

Cleve's brother, Joe, and their stepfather, Bob Blount, decided to purchase a Ford automobile. Rather than ride in the new mechanical contraption, Mother Mary decided that she, Buster, and Cleve, would drive to Phoenix in a horse-drawn buggy. Buster had saved enough earned money to purchase a bicycle and he rode alongside the buggy.

In Phoenix they went to Jerry Doyle's auction and Cleve purchased a motorcycle. Once he had ridden it home, he decided it needed an overhaul. All went well on tearing the engine down. But when he attempted to put the engine back together he had a number of parts remaining; enough that the machine would not run. He never did get it put together again.[9]

Later they moved to Cashion, Arizona. Cleve began the practice of "girl dating" while living there. He and his brothers triple dated as the three sisters they were dating had a car. They had dinner one night at a fancy eating establishment in Phoenix and one of the girls ordered lobster tail. She didn't know what it was and couldn't eat it. All three boys had to dig deep in their pockets to pool their money and come up with enough to pay the bill.[10]

Later, Cleve left on his own to Pleasant Valley, Young County, Arizona. He stayed there for a year with a twenty-acre place and about ten horses. That was in 1920 and according to Cleve "I had a good time."

There was only one place to go to dance and that was at the schoolhouse. "Them old gals would come from everywhere, come running to those hills in high gear. But had loads of fun."

Cleve went back to Phoenix in 1921 and he and Bob Blount ran cattle up on the Agua Fria River below Pleasant Lake Dam in 1922. Cosbia Janes lived above Pleasant Lake and Cleve became stuck on her. Cleve said that was before they built the dam. He had an Oldsmobile with an eight-cylinder engine that got about ten miles per gallon, and he would drive up and he and Cosbia would go to dances, often staying all night and returning home the next day. In 1924 they married, and Cleve had $50 in his pocket. So as soon as they tied the knot, they jumped in the Big 8 and drove to the Fourth of July Rodeo at Prescott.[11]

That was all Cleve had to say about his life in Texas and Arizona. However, it is known that he made annual trips back to Kent County, Texas, for many years. A descendant was visiting Jeff D. Hardin's grave site in Clairemont one day and spied a pill bottle stuck in a crack near the headstone. There was a note in the bottle which read:

> Was here June 2, 1983 - age eighty-four, Cleve Hardin, son of Jeff Hardin & daughters Nita Beasley, Pat Lake . . . the address in Buckeye, Ariz. (too tired to look it up) . . . [brothers] Joe G. died 1972 - Buster Jeff April 1983, age eighty. I have been here every year for a long time visiting my father's grave, but I am getting old now and don't think I will be able to travel this far again. So, this is adios until we meet again.[12]

Chapter Fourteen
Undoubtedly, The Most Dangerous Man in Texas
By Norman Wayne Brown

This story was published by *The Tombstone Epitaph*. May, 2022 issue. *Reprinted with permission.*

In his autobiography *The Life of John Wesley Hardin As Written by Himself*, laid claim to being a cousin of Simp Dixon. Some descendants say, "I am one hundred percent sure they were cousins." Other descendants say, "I am one hundred percent sure they were not cousins." But they were.

John Wesley Hardin's mother was Mary Elizabeth Dixon Hardin, and her father was a second-generation Irishman named William A. Dixon. John Hugh "Irish Jack" Dixon was a third generation Irishman, and his sister was none other than Mary Elizabeth Hardin. Therefore, John Wesley Hardin and Jonathan Simpson "Simp" Dixon were first cousins. And, when it came to killing, Simp Dixon most likely far exceeded Hardin is the killing business.

According to Walter Dixson, author of *Richland Crossing*, published January 1, 1994, page 214, John Wesley Hardin went to visit his aunt, Susanna Anderson, a sister of his mother, and when he arrived there was another young man there who carried a brace of six guns. Mrs. Anderson said, "Johnny, meet your cousin Simp Dixon. But he spells it different."

She may have meant that he spelled his last name Dixson rather than Dixon. They shook hands and became friendly. They both stayed a few days and helped their aunt with a little farm work. While there, they got into a confrontation with a detachment of army soldiers. They killed one each, and the others fled for their lives. When Simp Dixon saddled up and departed his aunt's home, John Wesley Hardin said, "There goes, undoubtedly, the most dangerous man in Texas."

Simp Dixon was born in Porter, Green County, Missouri, in 1848. He appears in the 1850 and 1860 federal census records for Missouri. Simp, according to John Wesley Hardin and others, was a Klansman. Reconstruction in Texas was hard on southern whites for a number of years after the Civil War. The government's position was to punish them. Any unionist seemed to always be right and the confederate wrong.

The Lee-Peacock feud was a prime example of the wrongs done by the government by letting the Peacock gang walk all over the southern Lee clan. Many murders took place after the Civil War and continued into the early 1870s.

Three black men were accused of raping and robbing white women in and around Limestone County and the reconstruction government turned a blind eye to them. Not Simp Dixon. He waylaid them, shot and killed one man and hanged the other two.

It was rumored that Simp killed more than thirty men before reaching the age of nineteen. Simp Dixon put the fear into all black people in the region. They locked their doors and blew out the lights when darkness came. Others were so afraid to stay in their homes that they slept in the woods at night, returning to their homes only during daylight. It is unknown how many men Simp killed of the Peacock group.

Peacock and others wanted Simp Dixon dead, and a reward was posted. Simp's little brother, William "Billy" Dixon, was killed in the Lee-Peacock feud on March 6, 1868. He was eighteen-years of age. He was buried next to his parents in the Sears-Doss Cemetery, at Sears Chapel, Whitewright, Fannin County, Texas. John Wesley Hardin's birthplace was less than a mile to the east.

What led to Billy Dixon's death was caused by Elijah Clark. Clark was allied with the Peacock gang but had been a longtime friend of the Dixon clan. He came to the Dixon farm to call on the eldest Dixon girl, Hester Anne. She refused to have anything to do with him and made it very clear.

That enraged Clark and he stormed out the front door. In his haste, he forgot that he had left his pistol on a table just inside the front door. Hester's brother, Billy, had just ridden in and climbed down from his horse when Clark stormed past him. Clark then decided to vent his rage on Billy. Billy carried a pistol in a saddle holster on his horse and Clark went to the horse and pulled the pistol from the holster. He raised the pistol, pointing it at Billy and pulled the trigger. His aim was a bit off and the round missed Billy. Then, Billy quickly went and grabbed Clark's pistol from the table just inside the front door and blasted Clark out of the saddle and killed him.

A few weeks later Billy was on his way to Jefferson with a load of cotton. Some historians have written that he had a brother, Charlie Dixon with him. Others wrote that Charlie was a cousin and son of Doctor William Dixon who was John Wesley Hardin's grandfather.

The story was Billy and Charlie had to stop to repair a broken wagon wheel. They were approached by army soldiers and members of the Peacock gang. The government report says Billy was killed resisting arrest. According to Charlie the posse had taken the two without a fight and then shot Billy in the back, murdering him.

A reign of terror began around old Springfield when a young white man, known to the black people as "Dixie" appeared on the scene. Walter Dixson, in his book *Richland Crossing* stated that Dixie was thought to be a relative of Simp Dixon. That relative could have been John Wesley Hardin.

On the other hand, historian and descendant of the Dixon clan, Rob Cook, and historian Ronnie Atnip, believe Dixie was Simp Dixon. Hardin wrote that Simp was reported to be a Klansman and had killed thirty men. According to many, Dixie proceeded unrestrained to murder African Americans whenever and wherever he caught them. For more than thirty years a piece of rope dangled from a bending tree on the old Springfield-Groesbeck Road in Limestone County, Texas.

Legend has it that Dixie hanged two men known as Seymor Abrams and Norville Rhodes from that tree. This was first reported by Walter Cotton in his book *History of Blacks in Limestone County*.

Simp's half-brother, Dick Johnson, had gone to West Texas to keep out of the trouble but would come back later to try and protect his half-sisters who had been threatened by the Peacock gang. By 1868, Peacock and his gang had killed Billy Dixon. Then, Charlie Dixon was killed at Black Jack Grove, now called Cumby. It is claimed that Charlie and his father, John Hugh "Irish Jack," had started to the lumber mills near Winnsboro for lumber. Peacock and his gang followed them to Black Jack Grove and shot Charlie to death. His father brought the body of his son home in an ox wagon and buried him. There seems to be no evidence to support the existence of a Charlie Dixon as son of Irish Jack.

The time for a reckoning was about to descend on desperado Simp Dixon, the killer of many men and now twenty-one-years -old. The army ordered Sergeant Adam Desch, Company E., 6th Cavalry, stationed at Waco, Texas, to form a detachment of troopers and go on the hunt for Simp Dixon with orders to arrest or kill if necessary. The following is the action report submitted by Sgt, Desch:

> February 4th, 1870
> Capt. A. L. Bennett U. S. A., Acting Post Adjutant Capt. I have the honor to report that in compliance with Headquarters order, Waco Texas dated January 31st, 1870. I proceeded to Limestone County, Texas, and escorted my detachment at a convenient distance from the house where Dixon makes his quarters. I was informed by a colored man that he had returned to this house. I immediately started with my detachment to arrest him. At my arrival at the house he was in the yard. He had just turned his horse out and was going towards the house. As soon as he discovered us, he drew two six shooters and commenced firing at my men. I called on him to surrender but he paid no attention, but kept walking toward the house, seeing that he could not reach his house, he made for the woods. We, following him close and firing, driving the skirmish on to a road where a man was driving a four-horse team. Dixon called for the driver and threatened to kill him if he didn't cut one of the horses loose. The driver became frightened and ran from him. Dixon cut one of the horses loose and my men shot the horse. When within a few feet of Dixon, trooper Jackson stumbled and fell, and Dixon put his pistol to Jackson's head and pulled the trigger. Jackson

had reached up and grabbed hold of the pistol as the firing pin was stopped by his finger and prevented the discharge. Jackson them took the pistol from Dixon's hand and hit him in the forehead. The blow, plus my carbine, killed Dixon. He had been wounded five times during the skirmish. Guthrie, Jackson, Latham, and Hamilton acted with great coolness and gallantry. I left the body by the roadside near the home of Dick Oliver. I immediately returned to Waco.

The three soldiers Desch mentioned were William Guthrie, age twenty-three, from Ireland; James Jackson, age twenty-four from Ireland, or another soldier named Thomas Jackson, age thirty-five, from North Carolina. Also, William Latham, age twenty-four, from Virginia; and John Hamilton, age twenty-one, from Pennsylvania, or Manly Hamilton, age twenty-one, from Maryland.

Also, some historians have reported there were other men at Simp Dixon's house when he was killed. No others were mentioned by Sgt. Desch and it is very likely no others were there on

Simp Dixon gravesite was not in alignment with other stones. One could say he was buried crossed, as was his character. *Norman Wayne Brown collection.*

Closeup of Simp Dixon's headstone. The year of death and name Sim are wrong. *Norman Wayne Brown collection.*

that dark day.

According to the federal census of 1870 for Waco, Texas, forty soldiers in Adam Desch's company were white men. Two had families, twenty-three were foreign born, and the others were from Georgia, Illinois, Indiana, Louisiana, Maine, Maryland, New York, North Carolina, Massachusetts, Pennsylvania, and Virginia.

Someone wrote there was no Dick Oliver living near Simp's body that was dumped by the road, however, there was, according to the Freedman's Bureau, a Black man named Dick Oliver in Texas and there were many Oliver families living in Limestone County in 1870.

Simp's body was taken to Fort Parker Memorial Park at Groesbeck, Limestone County, and buried. His headstone simply reads Simp Dixon, 1872. Actually, it should read Jonathan Simpson "Simp" Dixon, Birth 15 Nov 1848 - 4 Feb 1870. He was twenty-one years of age.

Years went by until ladies of the community decided Simp needed a headstone. So, they had one made for him, but they were in error on his date of death with 1872 chiseled on the stone. But the young man buried in that grave was game and courageous to the end, and downright mean. Drawing two six-guns when faced with a number of soldiers with rifles and being wounded five times and still game until being killed, took a great deal of courage. As John Wesley Hardin said, "He was, undoubtedly, the most dangerous man in Texas."

Chapter Fifteen
A Lawman's Badge:
The Life and Death of Reuben H. Brown

By Chuck Parsons

One of the highlights of the 2009 WWHA Roundup at the historic Menger Hotel in San Antonio was meeting the artist Donald M. Yena and his gracious wife, Louise. Not only did he have on display the large painting which graces the dust jacket of Bob Alexander's book, *Winchester Warriors*, but he had several other mementoes from his amazing collection of Old West artifacts. The collection contains priceless objects such as the Captain Frank Jones Winchester when killed at the Pirate Island battle, but also his watch and chain, and his badge. It is always gratifying to see and at times even hold such historic objects in one's hands.

Another priceless relic from the Yena Collection is the badge of Reuben H. Brown, City Marshal of Cuero, DeWitt County, Texas, in the 1870s when the Sutton-Taylor Feud was raging. Unless you are a student of Texas feuds, and there were many, the name of Reuben H. Brown may seem insignificant, but he played an important role in the dealings of feudists who were intent on eradicating their enemies, by whatever means proved successful.

Reuben H. Brown's major accomplishment was the arrest of William "Bill" Taylor, who on March 11, 1874, in company with cousin, James Creed "Jim" Taylor, shot down and killed Bill Sutton and Gabe Slaughter, two members of the Sutton faction. Jim Taylor's pistol killed Sutton; Bill Taylor shot and killed his companion, Gabriel Webster Slaughter, who had done virtually nothing during the feud other than sign the 1874 peace treaty. The double killing occurred on the deck of the steamer *Clinton*, in the presence of Sutton's pregnant wife, and numerous other passengers. No one attempted to stop the pair.

Bill and Jim Taylor escaped that day and continued their lives as fugitives. Jim Taylor was shot and killed by a posse on December 27, 1875. After serving jail time, while waiting for trial and between trials, Bill Taylor apparently relocated to the Indian Territory of Oklahoma where he lived another fifteen years before he too was killed, or so it is believed.

R. H. Brown became a victim of the Taylor clan, his life ending on November 18, 1875, in a Cuero saloon. The law never identified his slayers, although there were several suspects, or "people of interest" as we would call them today.

The historic R. H. Brown badge showing he was City Marshal of Cuero, Texas. Topped with an eagle, the ornate badge is an impressive collector's item. Note the word "Texas" within the star. *Courtesy Donald M. Yena.*

Twenty years ago I was fortunate in being part of a small group who explored the Epperson-Brown-Jonischkies Cemetery in southern DeWitt County. Today it is a small fenced graveyard containing about three dozen marked graves, although the actual number may be twice that. One state historical marker proves the importance of the past: Allen Caruthers, a veteran of the Battle of San Jacinto, rests there as well as R. H. Brown, and members of his family.[1]

Reuben H. Brown was born November 28, 1851, the son of P. T. and Miriam Brown. The 1850 census, enumerated by A. W. Hicks, identifies the head of household as Palestearn, which may have been correct rather than a misspelling of Palestine, or a variant.[2] Enumerator Hicks spelled the mother's name as Myram. At this time their family included four children: Jesse K., age sixteen; Josephine, age nine; Bazil J., age five, and Joseph, one-year-old.[3]

A decade later the parents are identified on the census records as P. T. and Miriam Brown, the usual spelling now used, and the family has increased with the coming of Reuben H., followed by

John R., age five, and Allen W., one-year-old.[4]

The 1860 DeWitt County census is particularly revealing in that it shows the relationship of the Browns and the Eppersons. P. T. Brown's household is listed as number 43; the next household visited by the census enumerator, number 44, is that of Samuel Epperson. Both the heads of household were from Tennessee.

They both had left that state and lived in Mississippi; they then located in Texas. Not chance by any means, as Sarah Epperson's headstone shows her maiden name as Brown. Would that every headstone revealed the maiden name of the mothers. The Browns were neighbors in life, and some of them were virtual neighbors in death as well.[5]

By 1870 there were but four children living with P. T. and Miriam Brown: Bazil J., Reuben H., Joseph R. and Allen W. Living in the same household is now Amanda Foster, eleven-years-old, taken in perhaps to assist Mrs. Brown, now in her fifties, with no daughter to help in the household.

Between 1870 and the next census, dramatic events occurred to change the Brown family unit. Miriam Brown died on March 28, 1878. Born October 9, 1816, she had certainly lived a full life. During that decade Palestine T. Brown had lost one son and his wife. The troubles between the Suttons and the Taylors cost him his son.

As yet no photograph of Reuben H. Brown has been located. The recovered headstone provided an interesting addition to our knowledge, supplemented with the various newspaper accounts and recollections of men who survived the feud. Other than the headstone now unearthed in the Epperson Cemetery,[6] perhaps the only tangible item to mark his passing is the badge identifying him as the City Marshal of Cuero, Texas.

In the absence of a photograph we are fortunate to have one description of the man. Victor M. Rose, an early historian of the feud, who must have had at least a nodding acquaintance with some of the feudists, wrote that after the double-killing of Sutton and Slaughter, Brown "became the acknowledged head of the Sutton party. Mr. Brown was a young man, liberally educated, and almost a perfect specimen of physical manhood."[7]

We only wish Rose had expanded his acquaintance with R. H.

Brown, informing us what the middle initial "H" represented for example.

Early contemporary mentions of Brown include his participation in the signing of a peace treaty between members of the two fighting factions. On August 12, 1873, after a long preamble prepared by DeWitt County clerk, H. B. Boston, thirty-nine men stepped forward and signed their name to promise to keep the peace. Among those who signed on the Taylor side of the document were several who have since become well known in gunfighter lore: John Wesley Hardin; Mannen Clements; his brothers, James, John Gipson and Joseph Hardin. Kin by marriage was George Culver Tennille; two other kinfolks signing that day were brothers, Alf C. Day and Jack Hays Day. On the opposing side, Joseph Tumlinson was the first to sign, followed by eighteen others. The last to sign was R. H. Brown.[8]

What brought these fighting men together was the aftermath of Hardin's attempt to burn out Joe Tumlinson, a leader of the Sutton forces. Hardin had rejected the idea of ambushing his enemies along the side of the road on a dark night; instead he was going to set the Tumlinson house afire, then shoot its occupants as they ran out to escape the flames.

In August he gathered up his associates, and under cover of darkness surrounded the house. Their intent was to announce the day by throwing burning torches onto the roof and porch, thus forcing out whoever was inside. But when the attackers awakened Tumlinson's dogs, the plan had to be changed from the intended gun battle to a siege of the house. By this time however law-abiding citizens had learned what was happening and formed a posse, stationing themselves between the Hardin party and the house. They then convinced all involved to cease hostilities and with the peacekeepers keeping the two factions apart the three groups marched into town, where both parties signed a peace treaty at the courthouse.

Curiously none of the men signing were lawmen of any distinction. Who was the sheriff of DeWitt County in the middle of 1873, and why was he not present? Was there even a sheriff at this turbulent time? The appointed sheriff, John J. "Jack" Helm, had been shot to death by Wes Hardin and Jim Taylor the previous month; it was not until October 11, that a man named William J. Weisiger was appointed to replace him.[9] During this intervening period apparently it was every man for himself. Or, if there was someone considered the top lawman, he perhaps found it expedient to go pursue a fugitive in some far-off corner of the county when the likes of Wes Hardin and the Clements brothers rode into town. Significantly perhaps, neither Bill Sutton nor cousins, Bill and Jim Taylor, signed this initial treaty of peace.

But treaties sometimes merely mark a period of calm between two groups, allowing them to prepare for combat, and it proved to be true in this case. In late December of 1873, several men rode up to the Pridgen General Store in Thomaston, a peaceful village on the Cuero-Victoria road, and shot Wiley W. Pridgen to death. W. W. was a nephew of Senator Bolivar J. Pridgen, considered by many to be one of the leading spirits of the Taylor party. The treaty of peace now became a dead letter.[10]

By the end of 1873 the conflict between the two groups reached inside the town of Cuero's limits with members of each group firing at each other. Some members of the Sutton party were ambushed in the countryside, but instead of a hit and run raid, it became a skirmish, with the Suttons chasing the Taylors along the road to Cuero where the firing continued.

The Sutton party took cover in the Gulf Hotel while the Taylors found shelter in a building on the corner of Main and Evans Street. Finally, leading citizens again managed to convince the opposing groups to make peace, if only temporarily.

This second treaty of peace was signed by William Sutton and James Taylor; William Taylor did not sign, but perhaps he was not there. Neither R. H. Brown nor John Wesley Hardin signed, but a total of eighty-six men did. Although it may have involved men with the best of intentions, however, it failed to provide a lasting peace and became nothing more than a paper of historical interest.

The year of 1874 began with more killings, one by Marshal Brown himself. A large headline in the Cuero *Weekly Star* reflected the mood of many citizens: "WHO NEXT IS TO BE KILLED?"[11] The rhetorical question was followed by an account of three instances of recent violence. The killing of Armstead Johnson was reported, shot down in Clinton;[12] then the killing of McVea by Marshal Brown in Cuero.[13] Also, a man named John Kron was "dangerously wounded."[14]

Brown's victim was James Gladney, or Gladden McVea. The *Weekly Star* exonerated Brown, explaining the killing was "in sheer self-defense."

The *Star* continued:

> The affair created much excitement, as McVea was instantly killed. Everyone in the streets ran to the scene of death and horror which was in McGanan's bar room, [w]here lay the robust and stout form of McVea, who, a few minutes previous, had been seen on the street, sound and well, now struggling in his life's blood, to his heart's last pangs, in the firm grip of death." Judge Oliver K. Tuton conducted an inquest. The jury delivered a verdict of self-defense. "We were not able to learn the cause of this tragedy," continued the *Star*, "but understand that McVea struck the fatal blow on our Marshal, who is still suffering from the wounds he received on his head."[15]

Was the killing of J. G. McVea connected to the troubles of the Sutton-Taylor Feud? Jack Hays Day, a Taylor apologist, described Brown as a murderer, attempting to create the impression in the mind of his readers that those who sided with the Sutton faction were of an invulnerable group.

On March 11, 1874, the big killing occurred. William M. "Bill" Sutton and Gabriel Webster "Gabe" Slaughter, with Mrs. Sutton, several months pregnant, walked up the gangplank of the steamer *Clinton*, floating in the Indianola harbor, intending to leave Texas for the quieter plains of Kansas.

Their dreams of peace and quietude were shattered when Jim and Bill Taylor also walked up and challenged Sutton and Slaughter. They hardly had a chance to defend themselves, *but they were armed*. Nevertheless, both were killed. Jim now had carried out his vow to kill Bill Sutton, the man he believed was responsible for the death of his father and various other relatives.

When the widow Sutton, as well as the state, offered a reward for the arrest and conviction of the killers, Jim Taylor chose to leave the area and teamed up with John Wesley Hardin in Comanche County, over a hundred miles from the heart of the feuding country.

Strangely, Bill Taylor did not, perhaps believing he was invulnerable. He should have joined Hardin, as Marshal Brown intended to arrest him, perhaps out of altruism, but probably for the $500 reward. It now seems incredibly simple, as on April 3, less than one month after the double killing in Indianola, Reuben Brown arrested Bill Taylor — without gunplay! The *Star* reported the accomplishment, with large headlines, IMPORTANT ARREST!

> On Friday evening Marshal Brown arrested Bill Taylor, charged with having a pistol on or about his person. While the defendant was preparing to give bail the proclamation of Governor Coke, offering a reward for the arrest of Taylor, was procured and handed to the Marshal, whose duty it became to hold the accused for the charge of murder preferred against him (Taylor) by the Governor. The Marshal called the citizens to his assistance in committing him to jail. The citizens responded en mass. The next morning Taylor was sent, according to the purport of the Governor's proclamation, on the train to Indianola. It was thought advisable to send a heavy guard of citizens with the prisoner, in order that his person should be secured against both friend and foe, and that the law might take its due course.[16]

After this important arrest one might think Marshal Brown would have retained his position of authority and trust, but in June he resigned his position. The *Weekly Star* provided two small items to announce the decision, which do not seem to clarify the real reason. The first suggests he intended to continue his duties but that there was something improper in his qualifications. The single line read: "The newly elected town officers qualified last night – all except Mr. R. H. Brown."

In the same issue the following also appeared: "Mr. R. H. Brown tendered his resignation of city marshal on Monday morning [June 8]. Personal considerations prompted him. He served in the office to the satisfaction of all, and it is regretted generally that he resigned." So one continues to wonder exactly why Marshal Brown's term as Cuero city marshal ended so abruptly.[17]

Exactly what he did after he turned in his badge is open to

speculation. Robert C. Sutton, grandnephew of the slain Bill Sutton, as well as Victor M. Rose, suggested that Brown provided leadership for the Sutton party. If true, did Brown consider this a conflict of interest? More curiously, during the upcoming trial of Bill Taylor, his uncle, John Milam Taylor, was called as a witness for the defense. Brown now attempted to do away with J. M. Taylor, apparently believing he could board the train and raise a difficulty in which Taylor would be killed.

Author Sutton wrote: "When he [Taylor] and his Ranger escort boarded a freight train to return to Cuero, Rube Brown tried to climb on board also . . . he is supposed to have later apologized to McNelly and said that he was drunk at the time."[18]

Captain McNelly provided a lengthy report of his actions in DeWitt County, but he did not identify the man who attempted to board the train. He merely wrote, "On one occasion one of my non-commissioned officers was compelled to use force in ejecting one of the Sutton party, from a car on the Indianola R. R. into which he attempted to force an entrance for the purpose of raising a difficulty with one of the Taylors, who was being guarded to and from the trial of his nephew."[19]

Reuben Brown, if indeed he was drunk, had picked the wrong time to do away with Bill Taylor, as Captain McNelly never lost a prisoner once in his possession or in the possession of his men.

Bill Taylor was returned to Indianola to stand his trial. Sitting in a jail cell, he certainly pondered what his fate might be. If found guilty of first-degree murder, he would almost certainly be sentenced to hang. If found guilty of second-degree murder he would be looking at a long sentence, perhaps twenty-five years.Conversely, with the right attorneys and the right testimony, he would be found not guilty due to a plea of self-defense. And if found not guilty, should he remain in DeWitt County or leave the area like cousin, Jim Taylor, and John Wesley Hardin had done? Hardin and his brother-in-law, accused murderer J. R. "Brown" Bowen, now were enjoying new surroundings in far off Florida.

While Bill Taylor considered the future, nature played a hand in his favor. On the night of September 15, 1875, a hurricane struck the port city of Indianola. The waters of the Gulf of Mexico rose, threatening the town, but more importantly for Bill Taylor, the jail itself. Would the prisoners be forgotten and allowed to drown?

Calhoun County Sheriff Fred L. Busch[20] did not forget his duty; he opened the jail cell and, perhaps with several deputies, marched the prisoners to the courthouse. In theory the deputies would now guard the prisoners. But as the storm increased, they left their place of duty, perhaps to rescue endangered citizens. Bill Taylor and his companion-prisoner Joe Blackwell did just that, but no one can say with certainty how many lives were saved by the two prisoners, accused murderers. The storm began to abate on the seventeenth.

Calhoun County, Texas, Sheriff Fred L. Busch was elected December 2, 1873; re-elected February 15, 1876, and again November 5, 1878. He served until November 2, 1880. *Chuck Parsons collection*

The vigilance of the deputies was in name only, and two of the prisoners, Blackwell and Taylor, managed to catch the sheriff off guard and remove his pistol from its scabbard. Now armed, the two rode off on one horse. Knowing the horse with two riders would not last long, another mount was soon obtained.

Bill Taylor now was again a "free man."[21] Instead of leaving the country to perhaps find Hardin and Bowen, he returned to DeWitt County. Not only was that an unsafe move, but he further sent word to the former city marshal R. H. Brown that he intended to kill him.

Certainly R. H. Brown had heard threats against him before, and this one was no different, instead of hunting Taylor he ignored the threat. It proved to be a fatal mistake. According to one report, on the night of November 17, while relaxing in the Merchant's Exchange Saloon, he "was shot and killed by parties unknown. Five men entered the room at the same time, and each fired at him."

Two black men were wounded in the wild firing, one of whom,

Thomas Freeman, died from his wounds. Commented the reporter: "The general supposition is that it was Bill Taylor's crowd, as Brown was the officer who arrested him previous to his escape at Indianola during the flood, and it is stated Taylor sent Brown word he would kill him."[22]

A subsequent report provided some conflicting details: "Brown was sitting in a saloon playing cards, when a man walked in, took a drink at the bar, took a look at Brown and walked out, when immediately five persons came in and commenced firing at Brown. They then dragged him outside and shot him again."[23]

Whatever the details, Reuben H. Brown now was a corpse, another victim in the long-lasting feud between two groups in DeWitt County and the surrounding area. The next day his remains were carried to the cemetery some seven miles south of Cuero the event under the care of the DeWitt Lodge, I.O.O.F.[24]

Who killed R. H. Brown? Who were the five men? No one was ever formally charged with the killing, but certainly Bill Taylor and perhaps cousin, Jim Taylor, also were in the group. A later report suggested Mason "Winchester Smith" Arnold was the man "who fired the first shot at Rube Brown. . . "[25]

If indeed the two Taylors and Mace Arnold — and that remains speculation — were among the five, then logically the fourth and fifth shootists probably were A. R. Hendricks, a former McNelly Ranger, who had married into the Taylor clan, and perhaps Jack Hays Day, kinsman of the Taylors, and who later wrote a history of the Sutton-Taylor feud. Was the quintet who killed R. H. Brown composed of Bill Taylor, almost certainly; Jim Taylor, probably; Mace Arnold, reportedly the man who fired first; A. R. Hendricks; and Jack Hays Day?

The killing of Reuben Brown did not end the feud, but before the year of 1875 ended there was great damage to the Taylor cause. A posse under the leadership of DeWitt County Deputy Sheriff Richard B. Hudson surrounded three members of the Taylor party: Jim Taylor, Mace Arnold and A.R. Hendricks. A gun battle resulted ending only with the death of the three Taylor men.

The bodies of the trio were all interred in what is now the Taylor-Bennett Cemetery a few miles south of Cuero, where they now lay undisturbed. While R. H. Brown's headstone through the years sank into the soft earth, (but was later recovered), the stone of Jim Taylor stands tall and proud, with crossed Winchesters and a target at the top. Not many feet away are the replacement granite headstones marking the final resting place of Mace "Winchester Smith" Arnold and the former McNelly Texas Ranger, A.R. Hendricks. [26]

Ironically, of the various feuding men who brought sorrow to orphans and widows in the 1870s, a photograph of Bill Sutton remains; it is a keepsake preserved by the Sutton family protected now in the Texas Ranger Hall of Fame and Museum in Waco. The name of A. R. Hendricks remains simply a name, his unknown initials not giving a clue as to further identity, although his record of service under Captain McNelly remains in the Texas State Archives. But Reuben H. Brown's impressive headstone now stands proudly above ground, and his badge rests safely in a collection of one who loves the Old West in all its excitement, tragedy, and glamour.

Chapter Sixteen
George Culver Tennille, The Forgotten Feudist
By Chuck Parsons

This story appeared in *Frontier Times* publication, Dec.-Jan, 1976 as "Forgotten Feudist."

George Culver Tennille [also recorded as Tennelle] gained little fame or notoriety during the violent years of the Sutton-Taylor feud in Texas. John Wesley Hardin, James Creed "Jim" Taylor, William M. "Bill" Sutton, and John Jackson Marshall "Jack" Helm, — all gained a certain degree of immortality in the feud literature because of their violent deeds. Tennille did not. He was present during the bloodshed, but he kept in the background, perhaps acting more as an advisor to the young guns than a gunfighting participant.

He should not be forgotten, however, for he died violently because his kith and kin were allied to the Taylor family when it was almost an impossibility to remain or even act neutral. Numerous others met that same violent fate during the feuds which plagued Texas during the post-Civil War Reconstruction period and beyond.

Little is known of Tennille's early years. He was born in Saline County, Missouri, on December 29, 1825, when that part of the country was still the frontier. The family, Tennille Sr. and his wife, Sarah Elizabeth Davis Tennille, immigrated to Texas with Stephen F. Austin's third colony in 1826. Twenty years later George Jr. married Annastatia Brown, but the marriage was short-lived. On July 7, 1853, he married Amanda Jane Billings.[1]

Tennille had a better education than most of his contemporaries and obtained a degree to practice law. He taught Amanda to read and write. Apparently, his father died about the time of the second marriage, and his land passed to his son. An early record shows George, Jr. deeding 326 acres located on the north side of the Rocky, a branch of the Sandies River [or Sandies Creek], to Andreas Duderstadt for $407.50. The deed was recorded February 27, 1858.

This deeding of land brought two frontier families together; a daughter of George Tennille Jr., Henrietta, would marry not too many years later a son of Andreas Duderstadt, Fred. Fred would essentially avoid the violence of the feud, although he became a good friend of the man-killer John Wesley Hardin.

The Civil War forced all able-bodied men to change their plans. Tennille enlisted in the 2nd Regiment of the Texas Infantry, under Colonel J. C. Moore

Feud victim George Culver Tennille. He lost the gunfight when challenged by a Gonzales County posse. *Chuck Parsons collection.*

and Captain G. W. Fly for the duration of the war. Private Tennille received a furlough to visit home in January 1862. Confederate records in the National Archives reveal he deserted January 20, at Houston and was still "absent without leave" in February. Why this misunderstanding took place is learned from additional documents in the file. It was a case of inadequate communication.

Tennille had broken a leg in 1846. For many years he was unable to walk for any length of time or much distance. When he enlisted, he received assurance that he could be transferred to the cavalry since he was unable to drill but little. The arrangement was that if he, Tennille, could get two able-bodied recruits to replace him, his transfer to the cavalry would automatically follow. With this in mind Tennille returned home.

At a cost of $100 he provided two young men to take his place and mailed their oaths, with his transfer request, to Captain Fly. Tennille's furlough expired before he received a reply, and since he had not returned to camp he was listed as a deserter.

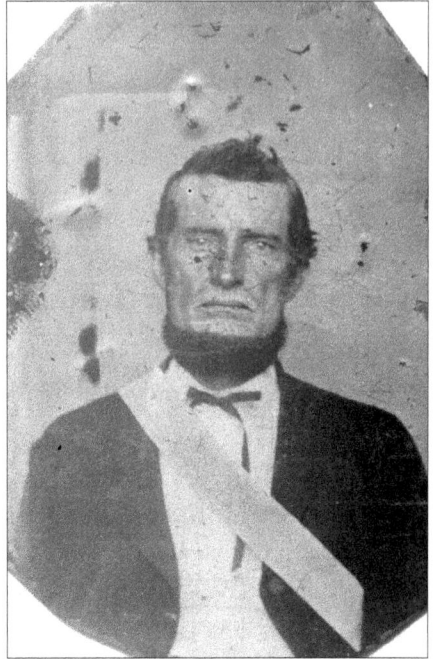

Tennille was arrested and confined at Camp San Antonio, along with a Private Simpson. Three letters are on file, two dated May 23, 1862, the third undated, explaining the details of why he was considered AWOL. The letters were written by E. F. Gray, T. N. Waul, and S. N. Conley. Just how this misunderstanding was worked out is not recorded. Whether he was transferred to the cavalry, or remained in the infantry, or what action he did see in the war remains unknown.

After the Civil War ended, Texas was to suffer through long years of political, economic, and social turmoil. Much of the state was still in a frontier-like condition. A great deal of racial and political animosity prevailed throughout. Under Governor Edmund J. Davis a bill creating a State Police force was passed on July 1, 1870. Its purpose was to reduce lawlessness, but the force was never accepted by the majority of Texans; partly because many of the policemen were black.

This Reconstruction period marked the beginning of hostilities which would become known as the Taylor-Sutton feud. No one cause can be identified as more significant than another, although the actions of the State Police force and one of its captains — Jack Helm appear to have been the most detrimental to any possible early solution.

George Tennille's actions in the early years of the feud have not been recorded but we may assume that he at least sympathized with the Taylor group. It is not our purpose here to defend either faction or to condemn one more than the other. Victor M. Rose, editor of the influential *Victoria Advocate*, (still published in Victoria, Victoria County) who was in a position to know a great deal about the trouble, wrote the first account of the feud. It was published by a New York publishing house in book form in 1880.[2] Since then, many other books and articles have been written, none of which agree in all respects. The following, therefore, is offered simply as a background for the circumstances which destroyed George Tennille.

During the summer of 1866, Charles Taylor was arrested for horse stealing by a posse which included Bill Sutton. He was killed supposedly when he attempted to escape. A few months later Buck Taylor and a friend of his were killed by a posse, which again included Sutton. Editor Victor Rose implied that the Taylor family had no alternative but to declare war on the Sutton group; Jack Helm, a sympathizer of the Sutton force and deputy sheriff of DeWitt County, branded all Taylors as desperadoes.

During the late sixties Tennille kept comparatively uninvolved. Jack Hays Day, who was a feud participant and related to the Taylor family, wrote his version of the struggle in the 1930s but did not mention Tennille. Nevertheless, the latter had to have clearly indicated where his loyalty lay to incur the enmity of Jack Helm.

In 1873 a young gunman, who was a valuable man to have, allied himself with the Taylor side. He was John Wesley Hardin who had waged his own war with the State Police and was worth a sizeable reward.[3] Hardin was a frequent companion of Jim Taylor, [4] but it was not until 1873 that he became actively involved in the feud. He wrote a biased but, in many respects, a reliable autobiography in the early 1890s. In it is some information on Tennille, although brief.

According to Hardin's memoir, Jack Helm met up with Hardin for the first time in April 1873, although both knew each other by reputation before that. The two gunfighters wanted, at least on the surface, to come to an understanding. Probably Helm was nervous or scared of Hardin's fighting ability and wanted him to remain neutral if he would not join up with Helm's own forces.

Hardin said he agreed to meet Helm in Cuero, DeWitt County, to come to some kind of understanding. The two did meet, and Helm asked Hardin to join his company. Hardin said he and his friends wanted to remain neutral. These friends included George Tennille and cousin, Mannen Clements. A second meeting was planned.

If Hardin seriously thought he could remain neutral, it is surprising. He was well aware of the situation in DeWitt County and termed the Helm faction a "vigilant committee that made life, liberty, and property uncertain." He considered Helm the leader and Jim Cox, Joe Tumlinson, and Bill Sutton (all Sheriff Helm's deputies) as next in line. Hardin estimated the Helm force at two hundred strong.

Any thoughts of neutrality were certainly washed away at the second meeting. Hardin was accompanied by Tennille and Clements. At the home of Cox, where the meeting took place, Hardin was taken aside and informed that his legal problems with the law would be taken care of if he joined the Helm faction. Strings attached to this offer, according to Hardin, were some of Hardin's friends would have to be killed; and Tennille and Clements would also have to join Helm's forces or suffer the same fate.

Hardin listened and then informed his companions of Helm's plans. Obviously there had been little need to even consider the proposition.

Tennille predicted there would be an attack within a week. Hardin gives the date as April 23, 1873, that Helm and fifty men made a raid into the Taylor community. The men of the Hardin, Taylor and Clements households were all out cattle hunting, and Helm and his men reportedly insulted the women because they would give no information as to the whereabouts of Jim Taylor. After this incident the Hardin-Taylor group got down to some deadly planning.

A meeting was called at Mustang Motte. Hardin recalled that he, Tennille, Clements, and Jim, John, and Scrap Taylor were all present. The meeting proved to be productive, as during the ensuing weeks the Hardin-Taylor group took the offensive. It is uncertain just what role Tennille had in the bloody events which were to follow, but if he was not actively participating, he at least knew of them. Most likely he was involved in the planning.

On May 15, Jim Cox and Jake Christman were killed from ambush. Two days later Helm himself was killed by Hardin and Taylor in Albuquerque, in Gonzales County, as Hardin recalled.[5] The next day the Tumlinson and Hardin forces came close to a battle, but the leaders were induced to form a truce. A "peace treaty" was signed at Clinton, on May 20. This was broken when Wiley Pridgen, a Taylor sympathizer, was killed, supposedly by Sutton forces.

It was not until March 11, 1874, that Jim and cousin, Bill Taylor, finally achieved their goal of killing Bill Sutton. On a steamboat at Indianola the two Taylors caught up with him as he was about to leave the country. Sutton and a non-combatant friend, Gabriel Webster Slaughter, died on the deck of the steamer *Clinton* in a brief exchange of pistol shots.

On May 26, Hardin and Jim Taylor, with other friends and relatives, were celebrating Hardin's twenty-first birthday in Comanche. In a street shoot-out Hardin and Taylor killed Charles Webb, the deputy sheriff of Brown County. The aftermath of the Webb killing was extremely bloody. It is difficult to determine if the revenge taken on Hardin kinfolk was because Hardin had killed Webb, or if it was more strictly limited to the feud-hatred proper.

Relatives as well as friends paid the supreme penalty during the following weeks. Joseph G. Hardin, Wes' older brother, and Bud and Tom Dixon, his cousins, were arrested, taken from jail and lynched the night of June 5. Two other cousins, Hamilton Anderson and Alec Barrickman, were shot to death as they lay asleep, if we can believe Hardin's version. Seven others were arrested while tending cattle: Jim White, Kute Tuggle, Scrap Taylor, James Bockius, Alfred Day, Pleas Johnson, and Pink Burns, and jailed in Clinton. During the night of June 20, before there could be a trial, Tuggle, White, and Taylor were taken out and lynched, the other four having escaped.

During this savage period Tennille is not mentioned as being actively involved but we can be assured that he was close by, as Hardin speaks of him as a trusted friend and companion. Shortly after he learned of the lynching of Taylor and the others, Hardin contemplated leaving the country, just as Bill Sutton had done two months before. He and a companion, Mac Young, went to Gonzales to say goodbye to a friend, Tip Davis.

Hardin wrote: "George Tennille went part of the way with us, and when we bid him goodbye it was for the last time."

He does not further elaborate on his friend's death or make mention of him again. We must presume much of the conversation on that way to Tip Davis's was how to avoid deadly ambushes from the Sutton sympathizers.

Tennille apparently planned to escape the feud's violence by leaving his home and hiding out in Mexico. He had made the necessary arrangements with a neighbor to sell his horses and turn the proceeds over to his wife and family to live on in his absence, but he was too late in his efforts to escape.

Only days after Hardin's departure, on July 8, a posse under Gonzales County's Sheriff William E. Jones caught up with him and he was killed — killed resisting arrest. The posse numbered about twenty-five men and had left Gonzales that morning. Some fourteen miles from town, about three o'clock in the afternoon, the posse reached John Runnels' house and there divided.

Tennille, having seen them from inside the house, rushed out and attempted to escape through a cornfield into some woods. The field was quickly surrounded. According to the sheriff's report, Tennille was repeatedly told to surrender.

A defective cartridge cost Tennille valuable time, for when his body was found a cartridge was lying by his side, with four or five indentations on it where the hammer had struck. Tennille had removed it, substituted another, and was again in the act of firing when he was killed.

Thus died George Tennille, surrounded by enemies, hopelessly outnumbered, but determined to go down fighting. Possibly he did not take part in many or any at all of the previous gunfights, but he was considered a dangerous man by the Sutton forces — one who had to be done away with. If he did try to stay neutral — and evidence shows that this was a distinct possibility — then his death merely proved that during the feud there was no way to retain a neutral stance — if a man were not for a certain side, then he was for the other side, in effect the enemy.

Tennille must have seemed quite out of place among the younger men of the Taylor faction. He was well educated, versed in law, and may even have been sort of a "father figure" during desperate situations. He was twice as old as many of them; for example, he was twenty-eight when Wes Hardin was born. His children were of the same generation as Hardin, Jim and Bill Taylor, and Mannen Clements.

A Texas Ranger who signed himself simply "Pidge" mentioned Tennille in a letter to the Austin, Texas, *Daily Democratic Statesman*, written November 12, 1874. He described how Hardin's forces surrounded Captain Joe Tumlinson's house and were preparing to set it afire when the timely arrival of the sheriff affected a compromise. It was a tremendously difficult job to gather a posse to prevent further violence, wrote Pidge "for was not Wes Hardin there? and George Tennell [*sic*]? And many more, who in the impressive language of this country, were 'bad ones'?"[6]

Tennille died at age forty-nine. He left a wife and six children: Amanda, Ann, Henrietta, Thomas, Harriett, and Nancy. Amanda, sometimes known as Sarah Jane, who married Joe Clements. Ann married Jim Clements, both brothers of Mannen and first cousins of John Wesley Hardin. Henrietta married Fred Duderstadt, son of

Andreas Duderstadt, from whom the elder George Tennille had originally purchased land on the north branch of the Sandy Creek.

With the killing of Jim Taylor and companions Mason "Winchester Smith" Arnold and A. R. Hendricks, in late December 1875, the feud began winding down. The killing of George Tennille was not the last death, and court battles would continue for many more years, but the general populace was no longer faced with choosing one side or the other.

Chapter Seventeen
The Grave of John Jackson Helm

By Chuck Parsons

This story was one of the chapters in *Captain Jack Helm: A Victim of Texas Reconstruction Violence* (Denton: University of North Texas Press, 2018). Copyright 2018 by Chuck Parsons.

Back in 1979 Dr. C. L. Sonnichsen, the *sui generis* of Texas feud historians, gathered together several essays which appeared in a book entitled *The Grave of John Wesley Hardin: Three Essays in Grassroots History*. They were entitled "Blood on the Typewriter;" "The Pattern of Texas Feuds;" and "The Grave of John Wesley Hardin." Each had previously appeared in highly respected publications, the former in *The Southwestern Historical Quarterly*; the second in *Observations and Reflections on Texas Folklore*, No. 37 of the Texas Folklore Society and the latter in *Password*, the publication of the El Paso County Historical Society. It is with honor and the highest respect that I acknowledge Dr. Sonnichsen and admit his title is the inspiration for this epilogue dealing with the burial and grave marking of the regulator Jack Helm.

The autobiography of John Wesley Hardin, published posthumously in 1896, provides a date for Hardin's killing of Jack Helm – May 17, 1873. (Of course, Jim Taylor should get the lion's share of the killing, but when Hardin was writing his life story, Taylor had been dead for two decades, so Hardin wondered, why shouldn't he take the credit? And he did but added Taylor to the final moments of Helm's career.) But the date of May 17, 1873, is incorrect, although we should not be too critical of Hardin's mistakes in memory: after all, a lot had happened in Hardin's life since the Helm killing and being off by only two months is certainly understandable. Unfortunately, that incorrect date has been passed down and numerous writers and historians have accepted Hardin's date and perpetuated the error.

Roy Sylvan Dunn in his "Life and Times in Albuquerque, Texas" accepted the date in his essay appearing in *The Southwestern Historical Quarterly*, published in July 1951; in so doing he unintentionally perpetuated the incorrect date. Dunn knew about the town of Albuquerque as he had grown up in Nixon, not far from where the town had existed. As an adult he became an assistant archivist at the Texas State Library; later, at Texas Tech University he was an associate professor of sociology and director of the Southwest Collection until his retirement in 1977. When the state placed two historical markers commemorating both neighboring Union Valley and Albuquerque, Professor Dunn was the honored speaker. Dr. James Smallwood, in his work on the Sutton-Taylor Feud entitled *The Feud That Wasn't*, perpetuated the dating error as "mid-May."

Descendants of Jack Helm have ignored researching the date to verify accepting what Hardin wrote as accurate, at least the date of his demise. Billie Rhoades Smith, great-granddaughter of Jack Helm and his wife, Margaret Virginia (Crawford) Helm, visited with Karon Mac Smith, Albuquerque historian and unofficial caretaker of the McCracken Cemetery. She intended to locate and mark the grave of her great-grandfather. In early 1973 she had come from Big Spring, Texas, to be present when the Confederate marker was to be laid in that rural McCracken Cemetery. The intent was to have the ceremony on the presumed anniversary of Helm's "untimely death." Miss Smith had read of the killing in Hardin's autobiography and accepted May 17, 1873, as the correct date.

Two historical markers near the intersection of the road which lends to the McCracken Cemetery remind travelers that Albuquerque once existed. Near this site was the village which was also remembered that day Union Valley. As Professor Dunn had been at Texas Tech, it was only natural that a Lubbock newspaper would report this significant event. "It was in the Albuquerque blacksmith shop that Hardin shot DeWitt County sheriff, Jack Helm, in 1873. The Albuquerque settlement faded when residents moved to Union as it was settled. Union in turn dwindled away when bypassed by the Galveston, Harrisburg and San Antonio Railroad."

The ceremony was held on Sunday June 11, 1972. Dunn's speech is preserved as "Historical Marker Dedicated — Union

Valley Homecoming" in Karon Mac Smith's *On the Watershed of Ecleto and Clear Fork of Sandies*. Lubbock had received a copy of Dunn's speech prior to the event and headlined its article, "Dedication Set for Markers" in the *Lubbock Avalanche-Journal*, Saturday June 10, 1972, issue.

About 1967, Karon Mac Smith took over the task of keeping the cemetery as her aunt, Karon Smith, and Clyde Hastings had done before her. She and friend, Gerry Sparks, placed a small concrete slab on Helm's final resting place, replacing the red boulder.

In 1973, Billie Rhoades Smith, the great-granddaughter of Jack Helm, visited Karon Mac Smith in order to personally visit Helm's grave. She ordered, and received, a free government headstone after proving she was kin to the veteran; she was assisted in this effort by Karon Mac Smith due to her efforts in caring for the ceremony. This was in January or February of 1973.

Using the incorrect date of Helm's death as recorded in Hardin's autobiography as well as other historians who have accepted that date, Billie Rhoades Smith and her two daughters, China and Cinnamon, and others had a brief ceremony at the placing of the government marker. The historic event was one hundred years following the death of Helm; that it was a few months off from the actual centennial of his passing was certainly not realized by anyone.

Today, unless the ceremony has been recently mowed and cleaned, the two grave markers of Jack Helm are difficult to find. Karon Mac Smith inventoried the graves in preparation for her books and included the grave of Margaret Virginia (Crawford) Helm, Jack's second wife. She gave the dates of her life as 1839 and March 18, 1877. Somewhere she had found a notice of her passing, but today her source is unattainable. We must accept that four years after Jack's burial, the earthly remains of his widow were placed next to that red boulder in the McCracken Cemetery

Today it is somewhat of an adventure just to find the grave of Helm. If one is fortunate to visit the landowners and get permission to visit the McCracken Cemetery, or "Old Albuquerque Cemetery," having the key to the gate will save many yards of walking. Once inside the pasture — and be sure to lock the date behind you — one must walk quite a way over rough pastureland.

If not found after a hundred yards or so, one must look around

Karon Mac Smith at the grave of Jack Helm in the remote rural McCracken Cemetery in northwest Gonzales County, Texas. *Chuck Parsons collection.*

and explore; eventually the cemetery will be found. Then enter through the falling fence and walk a few rods to the right, and hopefully the grass will not have stretched its leaves over the flat marker covering them from view — there are two of them. If you find one, you are fortunate; if you find both you are very fortunate. You have found the grave markers of John Jackson "Jack" Helm.

Chapter Eighteen
A Note on "Shorty" Anderson
Witness to the Killing of John Wesley Hardin

By Chuck Parsons

Readers of the *El Paso Herald* on August 20, 1895, learned that "Shorty" Anderson, real name Isaac E. Anderson, *AKA* Charles Richards, had been in the Acme Saloon on the corner of Mesa and San Antonio streets the night before and witnessed one of the most historic events in western history. In that saloon were John Selman Sr., E. L. Shackelford, Henry Brown, several others and of course the notorious ex-convict but now attorney at law — John Wesley Hardin. The biggest event of Texas that night was when Constable John Selman killed Hardin. Selman believed it was a case of "kill or be killed" and shot first. What is our concern here is the statement of Anderson, who testified before Justice Walter D. Howe in the investigation of Hardin's death:

> I watched the boys shaking dice in the glass. Pretty soon Shackelford and Selman came in — they had gone out and went to the bar and took a drink. I got up from the table then and walked about three feet from the inside doors. I saw Hardin turn and throw his hand back upon his hip, throw his coat back. Then I heard a pistol shot and he fell. I don't know who fired that pistol shot. I did not hear anything said when that shot was fired. Three or four shots were fired. When the smoke cleared up, I saw Hardin lying on the floor, and John Selman and his son in there.

According to Anderson's testimony, Hardin was in the act of going for his pistol to shoot Selman when he was hit. He happened to be just a mite slow against the constable. According to the several doctors who examined his body, Hardin was hit in the back of the head, in spite of the evidence of the photograph which shows a neat bullet hole above the left eye.

But that was not a concern of Shorty Anderson. In this situation of Anderson being in the same room as John Selman, did he not recollect that a few years before he was *in durance vile* because of Selman's, and a few others', tracking ability to rundown horse thieves? This aspect of Shorty Anderson's life is of our concern here, as well as his passing a few years after the memorable night in El Paso's Acme Saloon.

"Shorty" Anderson has long mystified researchers who intend to learn everything possible regarding John Wesley Hardin. By accident, while searching for something else, we came across information about the man previously forgotten. Learning more about Shorty Anderson proved to be enlightening indeed. He died as violently as did Hardin, but today he is nearly unknown.

We have learned that at birth "Shorty" was given the name of Isaac E. Anderson by his parents, Alexander L. and Christina A. Anderson. In 1870 Federal Census taker, W. H. Clark, enumerated the family in their Kansas home: Alex. L. was from Ohio; Christina A. from Pennsylvania; their first three children — John, Earl and Isaac — who will become known as Shorty, were all born in Ohio.

Sometime after Isaac's birth in 1864 the family left Ohio; they are next found in Ottawa City, Franklin County, Kansas, where by 1880 the family will have increased with daughter, Grace, sons, Alexander B., and Evin. The family appears to be well off; the 1875 Kansas Territorial Census shows the head of household claiming real estate valued at $3,500 and personal estate valued at $6,000.

He was obviously successful in his occupation of hardware merchant. By the time of the 1880 Federal Census, he is identified simply as a merchant. His three oldest sons, John B., R. Earl, and Isaac E., now are listed as clerks, presumably working for their father.

Due to the loss of the 1890 Federal Census many questions concerning Isaac E. Anderson which could have provided us with answers are unobtainable. We do know that during the 1880s-decade Shorty left his home in Kansas. No trace has been found in Kansas records as to why, but while business went on in Franklin County, Kansas, for the Anderson family — Shorty found getting off the straight and narrow in El Paso County, Texas, was easy. He was working both sides of the Rio Grande and working both sides of the law-and-order coin.

The *El Paso Daily Times* of June 20, 1891, gives the disturbing account of Anderson, now clearly miles away both physically and spiritually from his parents' influence. "Smugglers Run Down" read the initial headline, followed by a detail from the article that law officers had recovered eighty-six head of smuggled horses. We learn that on May 28, 1891, custom agent, Frank R. Clark, United States agent Irwin, and officers W. T. Kitchen and Stevens in company with U.S. Deputy Marshal Bob Ross, inspectors John Selman, J. C. Jones and John Ford had left El Paso in an attempt to capture a "daring band of smugglers" led by Shorty Anderson and Sam Brown. One hundred fifty miles out on reaching Penasco in the Sacramento Mountains they stopped to give their horses rest as well as searching area ranches for smuggled horses.

At this point the hunters found a fresh trail as well as the spot where the rustlers had camped and branded the horses. Ross, Jones, Selman, and Ford having secured fresh horses pushed ahead on the trail, while the remainder of the group investigated the surrounding ranches. Here they recovered fifteen horses, acknowledged to have been smuggled over from Mexico. This group then headed back to El Paso with the recovered horses.

On returning to El Paso, they received a telegram from John Selman reporting from Amarillo, Texas, announcing that the trail from Penasco had led the pursuers to a bunch of seventy-one smuggled horses in charge of Shorty Anderson and Sam Brown. Both the notorious smugglers and the horses would be delivered to El Paso. The recovered horses were valued at $1,600.

Other than the census records this is our first discovery of the man Shorty Anderson — one time working as a clerk, but now a captured smuggler. It is mid-1891. On the night of Wednesday, June 24, Deputy Marshal Bob Ross arrived in El Paso from Amarillo with Anderson and Brown, the alleged smugglers. An *El Paso Times* reporter located Ross and learned how he had accomplished the capture:

> It was on the afternoon of the third day after we separated with Collector Frank P. Clark's party in Penasco where we took up a fresh trail that our party reached

Spring Lake, about 600 miles from El Paso and 85 miles from Amarillo. We had been riding hard living on dry lunches and were therefore very thirsty and almost completely fagged out, so we decided to go into camp and enjoy a lunch with coffee and take a short rest. Jones and Ford were to look after the horses, while Sellman [sic] and myself cooked dinner. The only fuel to be had was cow chips. Up to this time we had been sticking close to our guns but were so tired that we threw them under the wagon and Sellman and myself started out in opposite directions in search for fuel, while Jones and Ford proceeded to attend to the horses and then threw themselves down in a shade to rest. We saw a man some distance off on the prairie riding towards us but paid small attention to him. After a while I glanced up and laughingly said to Sellman that "Shorty" was coming after us. Four or five minutes later I looked up and saw Sellman walking leisurely toward the wagon but had no chips in his arms. I too started back with my chips and noticed that Sellman was working himself cautiously around to the rear of the wagon. I then looked up to the strange horseman who was not more than fifty yards away. He had been waved to come in and in responding he turned his horse so as to give us his right side just as a man would do who expected to fight. Up to this time I had not recognized the rider; but suddenly I heard Sellman call out "Shorty where is Brown?" I knew there was something up. "Shorty" dropped his hand for his pistol, but Sellman had his rifle down on him and made him drop his pistol and march into camp where I slipped a pair of handcuffs on him.

With Anderson captured it was a question of locating and capturing Sam Brown. Anderson acknowledged that he was in Amarillo with the horses. J. C. Jones then mounted Anderson's horse and made a hard ride to Amarillo. Once there, Jones met with Potter County sheriff, R. M. Warden, and explained his business. Brown was quickly and easily arrested without a struggle. Then the other lawmen with Anderson hurried on to Amarillo to join Jones, who had Brown. Now Ross, Irwin and John Ford, delivered prisoners, Anderson and Brown to El Paso while J. C. Jones and John Selman delivered the smuggled horses.

The afternoon of June 25, Anderson and Brown stood before Commissioner McKie for a preliminary hearing. They both entered not guilty pleas. They further asked for additional time to gather their witnesses. Their bond was placed at $500 each. During the hearing, Shorty Anderson recognized and joked with several of his El Paso acquaintances. The *Times* reporter noted he was "undoubtedly a nervy little fellow" who talked very "indifferently of the accusations against him."

Then on Wednesday, July 22, 1891, the pair had an additional hearing before Commissioner McKie who bound them over to await the action of the grand jury. We know little of Anderson during the next few months. A note appears in October that Sheriff Warden of Potter County arrived in El Paso on October 20, with an attached witness in the case against the two men.

In April 1892, their cases were continued. In May the five cases against Anderson and the four against Sam Brown were again continued. Then a final notice informs us that on August 9, 1892, Shorty "gave bond . . . in the sum of $1,200 and is now a free man. He gave a cash bond."

By June 1893, the five cases against Shorty were dismissed. The charges had been brought against the two men in June 1891, they were then arrested, but finally in June of 1893, Shorty Anderson was a free man. Presumably, Shorty behaved himself after this experience of being a hunted fugitive, arrested, and being a prisoner. He may have found a job and earned an honest living; and he may have also become a hanger-on at various saloons in El Paso, but at least he kept his name out of the El Paso newspapers.

On November 10, 1894, Alexander L. Anderson, Shorty's father, passed away in his home county of Franklin, Kansas. Did Shorty learn of his father's death and perhaps travel back home to be with his mother for a while? We don't know, but it seems that people in El Paso knew where he was from, and he could have done this.

Mr. Anderson, born April 22, 1834, and dying on November 10, 1894, certainly had had a good life, leaving a loving family to mourn the loss. He was buried in the Hope Cemetery in Ottawa, Kansas. Mrs. Anderson, née Christiana Peirsol, on December 9, 1834, lived long years after her husband's passing. She joined him on January 15, 1924. They had been married on September 12, 1859, in Union, Ohio. Mrs. Anderson is buried alongside her husband in Hope Cemetery.

* * *

Nearly a year later, in August 1895, Shorty Anderson, apparently now approaching what we might call "middle age," but living the life of a man with no past regrets or transgressions hanging over his head, could walk about the streets of El Paso a free man. It was the night of the August 19, when he entered the Acme Saloon, saw John Wesley Hardin throw his coat back, jerk his hand toward his pistol to draw it. But he was just a split second too slow, as then a bullet entered his head above the left eye, fired by the man now commonly referred to as "Old John" Selman, the same man who had arrested Shorty only a few years before.

Things eventually quieted down in El Paso after the Hardin killing. Old John Selman was to be tried for murder, but fate dealt a blow to the solemnity of El Paso's streets when Selman himself died in a burst of gunshots in the alley between the Santa Fe office and the Wigwam Saloon.

Selman and George Scarborough had argued inside the Wigwam but then took their argument into the alley. There it ended with Scarborough shooting Selman four times, from which wounds Selman died on April 6, 1896. It was only a little over a year after Selman had killed Hardin.

We don't know if Shorty Anderson had any thoughts concerning this latest killing. He may have been unconcerned with the violence of El Paso. Why should we be concerned now? After all he now had a job, living responsibly. He may have occasionally visited the Acme or the Wigwam but he was keeping his name out of the newspapers. We know that he worked for various El Paso businesses, driving an ice wagon; then a beer wagon for Houck & Dieter, also for Johnson & Co. He was also employed by a Mr. Nations to deliver meat and even on occasion drove cattle, although no one thought of him as a cowboy.

William E. Rhotan trusted him and hired him to operate his

THE MURDER.

A drawing of Shorty Anderson's murder. *Chuck Parsons collection.*

"Rhotan's Rest" spot in East El Paso on the road to Ysleta. Besides this work Anderson was also a member of the hook and ladder fire department. We have no picture of the building in which Anderson worked; he also slept there acting as a sort of night watchman. It was hardly an elegant place, but W. E. Rhotan trusted Anderson with keeping watch and handling the sale of wines, whisky, beer, cigars and various groceries. Because of this trust Anderson had not only a job but also a place to call home. He perhaps recalled when he was a clerk in his father's store, years before in Kansas.

But early on the morning of Monday, April 5, 1897, word reached El Paso via telephone that Rhotan's Rest had burned early that morning, totally destroying the building. By 9 a.m. the ruins were cool enough to enter what was left of the building. Rhotan and several others — now concerned about Anderson, as no one had seen him, as he usually joined them for breakfast, thought possibly he had been burned to death in the fire.

The men started going through the debris. They soon found the burned remains of Shorty Anderson: but only the torso and head as the "arms and legs having been entirely burned up." Why was not the entire body consumed by the fire? Those men investigating surmised that the head and upper torso were right up against a thin partition which cut his room off from the store proper. Against this partition were stacks of flour and corn sacks which had fallen over on Anderson's upper torso, entirely protecting that

THE BURNT BUILDING.

The burned-out building was the site where Anderson was murdered. *Chuck Parsons collection.*

part from the fire. Upon further investigation it was discovered that Shorty's skull had been cracked and the crack extended from over the left eye, going clear around in the right side to the back of the head. In addition, there were two large holes at the top of the skull, apparently made by some blunt instrument.

Dr. W. M. Vilas was called as well as several members of the fire department who removed the remains from the building. At first there was no clue as who had murdered Shorty Anderson and then burned the building to hide the crime. On the morning of April 6, Mr. Rhotan now considered the brutal fact that he was not only out of a source of income, but Shorty Anderson, his trusted clerk, had been murdered.

A hatchet had been found lying near Shorty's bed which Rhotan determined belonged to the building. Tracks were also found; following them they determined they were made by a large man and he had been running from the building.

The Rhotan roadhouse had been opened up only about three weeks before and was doing a "very fair business especially on Sundays." People going to Ysleta would frequently stop there and get refreshments. The night before the tragedy, Rhotan had been there to get the cash, which he took with him. If robbery had been the motive, the robbers would have been disappointed as there was very little cash remaining in the building.

There was no insurance. At this point the authorities could do little but notify Anderson's next of kin in Franklin County, his mother; she needed to inform them as to the disposition of the body. If she did not wish it sent home to Kansas, the fire department would bury it in their firemen's plot in Evergreen Cemetery in El Paso.

Dr. Vilas' thorough examination of the remains determined that the head had been crushed by a blunt instrument, probably before the burning. Soon afterwards the authorities had a clue to the mystery. Which officer should get the credit is undetermined, but a man was determined to be a person of interest. Joe Cooper, brought into the jail in a drunken state, admitted "that he knew who did the deed" and the officers were soon hunting those he identified.

While the wheels of El Paso justice were quickly turning a "subscription paper" was being passed through the fire department to raise a reward of $100 for the "detection of the murderer of Shorty Anderson."

At 2:45 p.m. on April 5, officers, Hernandez and George Herold, with several others had three men in their custody, charged with the murder of Anderson. Whatever techniques of questioning they had used was not revealed. The three men were Juan Levy, Francisco Frescas and Pedro Ruiz. This was quick work by the authorities. Arrests may have been easy; the action of a jury might take much longer.

The situation began with Joe Cooper, then in jail charged with drunkenness. He had come into town very drunk; several parties suspected he knew something about the fire. Finally, after "some time quibbling and dodging the questions he admitted to officers, Fernandez and Herold, that he saw the murder committed."

What Cooper described then was that there had been a party at "Rhotan's Rest" at which were some Anglos, some Mexicans, two Mexican musicians, Cooper himself, another American (Anderson) and the three men charged: Levy, Frescas and Ruiz. For an unexplained reason Cooper was kicked out of the party but instead of leaving merely hid himself by the back door out of sight.

Soon the musicians left. About daylight Cooper said he heard the remaining party members talking about killing Anderson. They initially talked of shooting him but decided against that due to the noise it would make. They then decided on killing him with the hatchet which was conveniently there. This they used; after the killing the body was taken into Anderson's room and placed on the bed. They then set fire to the house and left.

Cooper was quite drunk when he gave this account of what he supposedly had witnessed. Then Cooper, after leaving the building, met up with Pat Dunn, who determined Cooper knew something about what he dramatically — and drunkenly, described. Dunn then alerted the police. The trio of accused men were arrested that afternoon and delivered to jail. They were all very drunk and claimed they knew nothing about the death of Shorty Anderson.

Testimony from a drunken individual is always of doubtful value; our sources leave many questions unanswered, but a few newspaper items may provide a resolution to the Shorty Anderson mystery. El Paso residents may have quickly forgotten about the entire affair; after all, it did not involve a notorious character such as John Wesley Hardin.

During the late hours of June 17, 1897, the grand jury indicted Francisco Frescas, Pedro Reyes and Joe Cooper, for the murder of Shorty Anderson. This is a very unsatisfactory ending of our quest to learn more about Shorty Anderson. One additional item may be relevant: on Friday, November 9, 1900, a Mexican, identified only as Frescas and described as about forty years of age, died in his home and was buried in the Catholic Cemetery the following morning. Could he have been Francisco Frescas, one of the men charged with the murder of Shorty Anderson?

Some interesting facts have emerged:

Isaac E. "Shorty" Anderson is born in Ohio.

Anderson believed to locate to El Paso during the 1880s.

May 1891, Anderson is arrested for smuggling but comes clear of charges. John Selman is part of the posse arresting him.

November 1894 -Alexander Anderson dies in Kansas.

August 1895 John Selman shoots and kills John Wesley Hardin, witnessed by Anderson.

April 1896 - George Scarborough shoots and kills John Selman.

April 1897 - Shorty Anderson murdered.

January 15, 1924 - Shorty Anderson's mother dies in Kansas.

From the little that has been gathered about Shorty Anderson it is obvious he had lived a full and exciting life. He was, perhaps, as Othello, one that loved not wisely but too well.

Note: The newspapers spelled Old John's name as *Sellman* as well as *Selman*. The correct spelling is *Selman*.

Chapter Nineteen

James Monroe "Doc" Bockius
The Mysterious Little Man

By Chuck Parsons

First published in the *Newsletter* of the National Association and Center for Outlaw and Lawman History (NOLA), Spring, 1977, Vol. II, Number 4.

Although some of the Old West gunfighters sought and enjoyed the fame their exploits brought them, we must remember that there were many individuals who sought not the limelight, who tried to keep the peace, and who tried to manage their homes, care for their children, and live in obedience to the law.

But the Texas feud situation of the late 1860s and 1870s found a good number of men to take up arms against neighbors. And some achieved recognition for their acts, whether this recognition was sought or not. The feuds easily began between men for a number of reasons, such as disputes over ownership of cattle or horses, inadequacy of the law, bad memories from the Civil War and Reconstruction.

In that period of toil and tumult following the war's end a number of feuds originated, the best known involving the Sutton, Tomlinson and Taylor families. The popular press has published numerous articles and books dealing with the feud, giving attention to such individuals as John Wesley Hardin, Jim Taylor, Bill Sutton, and Texas Ranger L. H. McNelly.

The following biographical sketch hopefully encourages others to research the lives of lesser-known figures of that feud. One of those peripheral individuals of the feud was James Monroe Bockius, a little man known as "Doc."

In the feud literature his name is scarcely more than a footnote. Frequently it is misspelled, but this is not surprising, as people who knew Doc didn't always spell his name correctly. He never

did anything to gain such recognition as McNelly, Taylor or
Hardin did. Nor is there a record of his participating in any
of the Taylor ambuscades or
other shootouts which attract
the attention of modern historians.

Possibly he did not engage
in violent acts, but kept himself
busy with doctoring, or working
with the cattle herds of Gonzales County. Before we consider
the desperate escapades of the
feud situation, we will examine
his early life.

Where he was born is un-
certain, but possibly in the state
of Ohio, in the year 1831. Family tradition indicates that at
around the age of eighteen or

Portrait of James Monroe "Doc" Bockius
as an older man. *Chuck Parsons collection.*

twenty, he fled Ohio for some difficulty.[1] What exactly happened
will probably always be speculative, but by then he was a man
and could handle himself in frontier Texas.

The Texas military records provide additional information
concerning Bockius.[2] In the months preceding the outbreak of the
Civil War he was a member of the Mounted Rangers, Rio Grande
Regiment, commanded by the now famous Colonel John S. "Rip"
Ford, having enlisted February 23, 1861, at Banquette, Nueces
County. The record indicates he had been called into service to
serve from February 23 to September 13, 1861. Bockius was pro-
moted to sergeant on March 30, 1861.

He was mustered into the service for the Confederacy on September 14, 1861, at Brownsville, for a one-year period.[3] He was
thirty-years-old. Captain Mat Nolan was commander of this 2nd
Regiment of Texas Volunteers. Another record shows his being
mustered in at Point Isabel, Texas, on May 14, 1862, by a Lieutenant Rosenheimer.

One intriguing statement which begs for further information is as follows: "Entitled to $50 bounty May 14, 1862."

Bockius was close to some individuals who achieved considerable fame in Texas history. On March 18, 1861, an ordinance had been passed by the Austin Convention authorizing the recruiting of a regiment of mounted men for protection of the frontier, to serve for a twelve-month period. Ford was elected colonel, John R. Baylor lieutenant-colonel, and Edwin Waller major.

Ford's orders were to proceed to the Rio Grande, seize the munitions and arms of the United States government at Point Isabel and other points on the Rio Grande, and to put into effect measures necessary to protect the frontier. This meant not only protection from the Indians but from white and Mexican desperadoes as well, the most famous being the cattle rustling of Juan Cortina.

Whether Bockius knew any of these officers who did achieve fame or participated in any of the excitement on the border is not known. Certainly, if this period of his life had been recorded one could get a better glimpse into this mysterious figure. What he did to earn the $50 bounty is a mystery.

On May 4, 1863, Bockius was assigned to the customs house at Brownsville, on detached service for one year, by order of General J. Bankhead Magruder. One other document among the Bockius war papers is of interest regarding his parole. Dated at San Antonio, September 21, 1865, it states that Private Bockius of G Company, 2nd regiment, Texas Cavalry, Confederate States of America, was permitted to return to his home in Gonzales County, ". . . not to be disturbed by the United States Authorities, so long as he observes his parole and the laws in force where he may reside."

One story of his war experiences has survived in the family oral tradition claiming he was a spy behind Union lines. As the story goes, he hid and slept during daylight hours and did his spying at night. One place he chose to conceal himself was in a cemetery under a tombstone, with the grass concealing it, set up in such a way that a small man could hide underneath. One day he woke up in his hideout to find that a funeral and burial had taken place while he slept. People were looking at the various stones and reading inscriptions thereon. Because Doc Bockius was such a small man, he was able to avoid being detected. His diminutive size would save his life again later.[4]

From the war's end and until the mid 1870s he apparently was ranching or in some way involved in the cattle business. Although he was known as "Doc," he was not a licensed practitioner but knew enough medicine so that others depended on his knowledge and advice.[5]

One of Doc's Gonzales County acquaintances, if not good friend, was the well-known gunfighter John Wesley Hardin. It was because of Bockius's friendship with Hardin that he became involved in the Taylor-Sutton Feud and nearly lost his life to lynch mobs. Although Hardin was a man-killer and a wanted man, he was relatively safe in his home country. Others who resided there included Hardin's cousins, the Clements family, of which the brothers, Mannen, Joe, Gip and Jim, are fairly well known today. Of the brothers, only Mannen ever had real difficulties with the law.

Other cattlemen included the well-respected Fred Duderstadt, friend of the Clements brothers, and Ed and J.W. Glover. George Tennille, considered a dangerous ally of the Taylor family, was also a Bockius friend.

Apparently, the feud had begun in the Reconstruction years following the war and continued well into the 1870s. Although it is known today as the Taylor-Sutton Feud, only one Sutton — William, was involved. His brother James kept out of it. The Taylors were a large group who believed in settling their difficulties with a gun. Jim Taylor was considered the leader, especially after the murder of old Pitkin Taylor.

The chain of events leading to the near lynching of Bockius started when Wes Hardin's older brother, Joe, and Alec Barrickman discovered Bill Sutton's plan to leave the country by boat. The Taylors were alerted to this. What should have been the climax to the bloody feud was the double-killing of Sutton and his companion, Gabriel Slaughter. This occurred at Indianola on March 11, 1874. The feud did not end there, however.

Besides the herds being managed by the two Glover brothers and the four Clements brothers, Wes Hardin began an additional herd of one thousand head which he placed under the control of Doc Bockius. This was soon readied and was headed to Hamil-

Standing left to right: Mrs. A.E. Adamson, Mrs. Joseph Hardin Clements, Mrs. A.R. Treat. Seated: Mrs. Amanda Jane Billings Bockius, former wife of George C. Tennille and Frank C. Treat. When George was killed in 1874 Amanda Jane married Doc Bockius. Frank C. Treat is the boy standing next to her. *Chuck Parsons collection.*

ton, Hamilton County. Hardin was visiting his family in Comanche, some thirty miles west of Hamilton.

In the weeks following, the herds were prepared to leave for the Kansas markets, but Bill Taylor, constant companion of his cousin, Jim Taylor, was arrested by Rube Brown, the city marshal of Cuero. This prompted Jim Taylor to join Hardin at Comanche. Many of his friends, including Hardin, were leaving the country to head north, and he did not wish to be left virtually alone in enemy country.[6]

On May 26, 1874, residents of Comanche witnessed a pistol "duel" between Wes Hardin and Charles Webb, the deputy sheriff of neighboring Brown County. Neither man was alone, Webb having a dozen or more associates with him, Hardin having several friends and relatives at his side. Evidence indicates that Webb intended to kill Hardin and then he and the others could arrest Jim Taylor. But Webb died under the guns of Hardin, Jim Taylor and Bud Dixon, another cousin. Within moments the citizenry formed groups to pursue the killers.

The atmosphere was one of intense anger, and into it rode Doc Bockius, following orders of his boss, Hardin, to inform him when the herd was at Hamilton. He was immediately recognized as being a Hardin man and was placed under arrest, not because he had committed any wrong, but because he thus would be prevented from assisting Hardin, Taylor of Dixon.

Within days of the Webb killing, Joe Hardin, a Comanche law-yer and postmaster, along with cousins, Bud and Tom Dixon, were also placed under guard in the courthouse along with Bockius. The Texas Rangers who were there did not concern themselves with their involvement or non-involvement, as their interest was to cut Hardin off from friends and family, so his escape would be less likely.

Bockius was not charged with any crime but was still being held under courthouse guard eleven days later when a group of disguised men took over the courthouse and removed three of the prisoners: the two Dixon brothers and Joe Hardin. Bockius was not taken, nor were other Hardin associates who were being held: Jim Anderson, Thomas Jefferson Waldron (possibly Waldrip) and Will Green.[7] The three who were removed were hanged not far from town the night of June 7, 1874. Years later Hardin wrote in an affidavit:

> [Joe Hardin and the two Dixons] had been Surrendered to a mob on or about the 5th of June A D 1874 in the town of Comanche and county of Comanche and placed ropes around their necks in the court house and drug them bareheaded and bare footed a Short distance from town and their [sic] hung them until they were dead because J.G. Hardin [words ineligible] had the temerity to demand a Speedy and impartial trial for his brother and client from the officers of the law and that Tom Dixson [sic] was put to death because he was a relative of mine and eye witness to the homicide of Charles Webb.[8]

A contemporary described the excitement and violence as fol-lows, published in the *Denison News* and reprinted in the *Austin Daily Democratic Statesman* of June 17:

> Last Sunday night the citizens of Comanche took three prisoners out of the jail and hung them one mile and a half from town; their names were Dickson brothers [sic] and Joe Hardin, a lawyer of Comanche, and broth-er of J. Wesley Hardin, the notorious murderer who has killed twenty-eight men, is but twenty years old and

the son of a preacher. The sheriff with every available man in Comanche County is after him but to no avail. He and his party of seven or eight men fought forty men all day. Last Tuesday ten miles from Comanche on Leon bottom, he had his horse killed from under him. He is a fearless man, and I expect he will kill some more before he is taken. The authorities have his wife and child with his father, the preacher, in jail at Comanche.[9]

Ranger J. R. Waller with possibly thirty or more rangers had been stationed in Comanche. Thirteen of these rangers were ordered to arrest the other cowhands with the Hardin herd at Hamilton. Several of the rangers are known to us today: Sergeant J. V. Atkinson, William Green. Dave Hudson, Fayette Oxford. Years later Green wrote a valuable account of these violent days pursuing the Hardin gang.[10] The hands who were arrested, as best as we can determine, were R. P. "Scrap" Taylor, "Kute" Tuggle, Jim White, "Pleas" Johnson, "Pink" Burns, Alford and Charles Day, and the herd's cook. Hardin wrote in his autobiography that the latter three managed to escape at Hamilton.[11]

Bockius and the three Hamilton herd hands, as well as other prisoners, were taken by the thirteen rangers to Austin and then to Clinton, DeWitt County. Once there they placed the prisoners in jail but were warned by the citizenry that the prisoners would not stand trial. The rangers of course were merely following their orders to deliver the prisoners.[12]

Hardin viewed their action differently, writing that they placed the prisoners in the Clinton jail in order that the Tumlinson crowd, followers of Bill Sutton, could take them out and lynch them.[13] The *Cuero Star*, in an article reprinted in the *San Antonio Daily Herald* of June 30th, wrote that the victims were accomplices in the murder of Charles Webb.[14]

Whatever the reason, Taylor, Tuggle, White and Bockius were all removed from the jail at midnight on the stormy night of June 21-22, 1874. Bockius's small size and a friend's loyalty saved Bockius from the lunch mob.

One Joe Sunday, an extremely large man and a friend of Bockius, was there. He may have been present just to see what was happening, but for whatever reason, he was there, and lifted little Doc

This gang of cowboys worked for John Wesley Hardin according to Hardin. Actually, they worked for Mannen Clements. The identification came from the late Jack Caffall, who was related. Standing, left to right: Mannen Kimbro, Jim Denson, Ferd Brown, and James M. "Doc" Bockius. Seated left to right: Jim Clements, Joseph Hardin Clements, and Mannen Clements. *Chuck Parsons collection.*

Bockius behind him on his horse, getting him under his heavy wet slicker. The pair rode off to safety, while Taylor, Tuggle and White were hanged.

Just what Bockius did immediately after this narrow scrape, we do not know. Possibly he hid out in his home country, or possibly he headed for Kansas to be with friends, such as the Clements brothers, Duderstadt or the Glover brothers. At least in the Kansas cow towns he would be safe from the hatreds of the Taylor-Tumlinson feud.[15]

His friend, George Tennille, was killed within weeks, on July 8, 1874, dying a short distance from his home in a cornfield surrounded by enemies. Hardin fled to Florida where he remained a fugitive for three years.

Tennille's wife was Amanda J. (Billings) Tennille, and after her husband's death in 1874 she remained a widow for ten years. On May 10, 1884, D. D. Jones, Clerk of the County Court of Gonzales County, issued a marriage license to Bockius and the widow Tennille. They were joined in marriage three days later, May 13, by J. C. Gillespie, Gonzales County Justice of the Peace.

It was in the Tennille home that Doc established a post office, being appointed postmaster on January 19, 1885. Doc also became a "community consultant," especially for doctoring and delivering babies.

Sometime during this period, a sister visited him after some forty-five years of separation. Supposedly she was heard to remark that she could not understand why he had let the problem of his youth back in Ohio trouble him so.[16]

When John Wesley Hardin was pardoned after serving time for the killing of Charles Webb, he returned to Gonzales and renewed acquaintances. Of the Clements brothers who had driven herds to Kansas, only Gip and Jim were still in Gonzales. Joe had left for New Mexico, and Mannen had been killed in 1887. Fred Duderstadt still was there, as was Joe Sunday who had risked his life to save Doc Bockius.

Lewis Nordyke,[17] in his biography of Wes Hardin, wrote that Bockius was the presiding judge over the Gonzales County sheriff's race of 1894 between R. C. Coleman and incumbent Sheriff W. E. Jones. Jones won by only a few votes. Hardin had backed Coleman, and in this defeat, he left Gonzales and headed west to his eventual death at El Paso.

Doc Bockius died in 1909, at the age of seventy-eight. Although his name is virtually unknown today, he lived through the most turbulent times of Texas history; he was witness to the Civil War, to one of the worst of Texas's many feuds, and to the days when cattle were king. Had he chosen to leave a record, he might today be as well-known as Hardin and others of his group. He chose to leave well enough alone and tend to his doctoring and cattle herds.

Chapter Twenty
The Dangerous Career of Bill Taylor
Death in Oklahoma for a Texas Fugitive

By Chuck Parsons

This article first appeared in *"OKOLHA"*, the publication of the Oklahoma Outlaws Lawmen History Association, Vol. VII, No. 4, Winter 2010.

Bill Taylor rode out of the flood waters of Indianola, Texas, making his escape from Calhoun County Sheriff Fred. L. Busch. Did he continue a life as a hunted man, eventually leaving his native state to finally die mysteriously in the Indian Territory of what is now Oklahoma? Or was his supposed death only a ruse to allow him to live peacefully the rest of his natural days? The answer is not yet solidly determined, but perhaps a member of WWHA can help resolve the problem. His days of peaceful growing up to a violent adulthood are fairly well preserved thanks to court records and contemporary documentation. What about his last day on this earth?

Bill Taylor remains one of the leading figures of the 1870s in Texas feuding history. A dangerous man, he was willing to use his guns to settle difficulties or simply to assist a family member to gain revenge. His early years were spent on a DeWitt County farm, mastering perhaps the needed knowledge of stock-raising during the years before barbed wire, as well as the use of pistol or gun. History knows him best as the man who killed Gabriel Webster Slaughter, while his cousin killed the leader of the forces fighting the Taylor clan — William M. Sutton.

The subject of our sketch was named after his grandfather, William Riley Taylor. The patriarch of this branch of the family tree was born February 9 (or 16), 1811; he passed on January 12, 1850. His wife was Elizabeth Tumlinson (July 13, 1814-February 22, 1886). W. R. Taylor was a native of Clarke County, Georgia; his

wife a native of Tennessee. This
couple gave nine children to the
world, two of whom died by violence.

Their first-born son was
named Creed, killed in 1854 by
his brother-in-law — William
Ainsworth.[1] A brother of Creed,
William P. "Buck" Taylor, was
killed Christmas Eve 1868, in a
difficulty with William Sutton
and others. A cousin of Buck
Taylor, Richard Chisholm, died
in the same encounter.[2]

Creed Taylor and his wife,
Eliza Ainsworth, were the parents of William Riley Taylor, the
subject of this sketch. His exact
birth date eludes us, but sometime in 1851. The 1860 Federal

The dangerous Bill Taylor whose fate remains a mystery. *Chuck Parsons collection.*

Census shows the widow Taylor, forty-one years of age, in household #312, DeWitt County. Son William, five years of age, is living
"next door" in household #313, living with Joseph and Martha
McCartney.[3]

During this decade, besides the difficulties of surviving in a
Confederate state in war time, with Union forces threatening on
the east and potential Indian raiding parties on the west, the Taylors experienced tragedies first hand: brother Buck lost his life
to the Sutton forces; two other cousins, John Hays and Phillip
"Doboy" Taylor, killed two Union army men near Fort Mason,
making them fugitives from justice with a large reward offered for
their death or capture.[4]

In 1870, working on the Elizabeth Taylor family farm, census
enumerator, Willis Fawcett, visited the household. Fawcett enumerated Mrs. Taylor as a widow, occupation given as farming with
real estate valued at $1500 and personal estate valued at $3200.
Living with her was daughter, Eliza Jane, thirty-two, William Riley, fifteen, a "farm hand" and the younger son, James, nine years
of age.[5]

In his mid-teens in 1870, Bill Taylor apparently had done nothing to attract the attention of the authorities. At least no contemporary account is known to exist placing him on the wanted list of a lawman. But the troubles with the law were not far in the future for Bill Taylor, and the troubles between the Taylors and the followers of William M. Sutton would increase.

In fact, Bill Taylor may have spent the rest of his life working on his mother's acreage if not for his involvement with a cousin, James Creed "Jim" Taylor. The two cousins had one tragic thorn in common, other than feuding blood running in their veins. Bill's father had died violently, whether in an ambush or in a face-to-face confrontation is unknown; and Jim's father, Pitkin Barnes Taylor, was killed in an ambush, shot down in the night by unknown parties as he was called out from his home to investigate a suspected theft of the family cow. He took several months to die from the wounds he received.

That alone made the two Taylors bound for revenge. No one was ever brought to trial for the killing of Pitkin B. Taylor, but in the mind of the Taylor clan the guilty man was William M. Sutton. They had little, if any faith in the court system, choosing instead the Old Testament law of vengeance, ignoring the Lord's admonition completely: "Vengeance is mine; I will repay."

At the funeral of Pitkin Taylor in March of 1873, in the small cemetery south of the county seat, Cuero, DeWitt County, on the banks of the Guadalupe River, Jim Taylor vowed to avenge the death of his father. His mother held up well under the strain until the mourners heard and observed from across the Guadalupe River the ribald celebration of a group of men, followers of William M. Sutton.

Was Sutton actually there, across the river from the cemetery? No one can say for sure today, but the Taylors *believed* he was there, which marked him for death in the mind of Jim Taylor. Taylor made an oath to wash his hands in old Bill Sutton's blood. Jim Taylor certainly was speaking figuratively rather than literally, but the end result would be the same.[6]

William Sutton was stalked by Taylor. How many times a Taylor ambush was planned and failed is unknown, but Jim Taylor was a determined young man. The attempts and efforts finally bore fruit on the 11th of March 1874 at Indianola, Calhoun County. Sutton, in company with his wife, Laura, now perceptively pregnant with their first child, and friend Gabriel Webster Slaughter, descended from a hack to walk up the gang plank to board the steamer, *Clinton*. There were other acquaintances present. But there were two others who within moments also walked up the gang plank.

Jim and Bill Taylor had finally caught up with Bill Sutton. Jim Taylor challenged Bill Sutton and the gunfire began; Gabe Slaughter now attempted to defend himself from the guns of Bill Taylor. Both Sutton and Slaughter were killed, their weapons having done no damage to the Taylors. Amid Laura Sutton's screams and the echoes of the pistol shots, Jim and Bill Taylor ran to their positioned horses and made their escape from Indianola.[7]

The double-killing resulted in the widow Sutton as well as the state of Texas offering a $500 reward for the men who successfully killed the two men. In addition, this double-killing brought enough attention in the governor's office that plans were made to activate a militia unit to be sent to DeWitt County, considered by many to be the center of the feudists' activities.

Jim Taylor wisely removed himself from the area, joining up with John Wesley Hardin to drive cattle to the northern markets. Bill Taylor, unwisely, chose to remain in the immediate area.

In spite of how the western movies have portrayed the Wild West, most communities, such as Cuero, Texas, had ordinances forbidding wearing guns inside the town limits. Many individuals did not wear arms of any kind, others wore them concealed. How Bill Taylor wore his pistol is unknown, but city marshal Reuben H. Brown observed him with a pistol as he was trying on a new pair of boots in a Cuero general store. Marshal Brown arrested him without incident apparently both men figuring Taylor would pay his fine and go on his way. But someone reminded the marshal that there was a reward offered for Taylor, on the much more serious charge of murder.

The authorities determined Bill Taylor was too dangerous a prisoner to be confined in the local jail, so he was transported to the much stronger jail in Galveston. When his trial was called, he was taken to Indianola where the crime had occurred and jailed. But nature had other plans, as a hurricane now rose, causing many to fear for their lives from the rising waters of the gulf.

Whether it was the Calhoun County marshal, Fred L. Busch,[8] or a judge is unknown, but someone had the foresight to remove the prisoners from the jail and escort them to higher ground. Reportedly prisoner Taylor and one other, Joe Blackburn, actually helped save several lives by rushing into the rising waters at the risk of their own lives. As the storm abated, Taylor and Blackwell saw their opportunity, took the pistol from a deputy, stole a horse and rode away double. In a short time, they obtained another horse, leaving an embarrassed group of authorities without two important prisoners. What happened to Blackburn is unknown.[9]

Bill Taylor, now a "free man," could not leave his home country; but more importantly, as his cousin had vowed to avenge his father's death, Bill Taylor now vowed to kill Reuben H. Brown, the man who had arrested him. Reportedly he even sent word to Brown that he would do so. The night of November 17-18, 1875, Rube Brown chose to enter into the Merchant's Exchange bar in Cuero where he began playing cards. This was the night that the Taylors achieved their purpose: someone entered into the bar, noted Brown was present, went back outside and within moments guns roared.

Rube Brown was instantly killed, while two black men were wounded; one of them named Thomas Freeman, died from his wounds. Brown's corpse was carried away and buried in the family cemetery some eight miles south of Cuero. No one was ever charged officially with the killing, but it was the general belief that Bill Taylor was one of them; Jim Taylor was likely there, as were several others whose names were associated with the Taylors: A. R. Hendricks, Mason "Winchester Smith" Arnold, and Jack Hays Day.[10]

Vengeance followed: on December 27 a posse surrounded Hendricks, Smith and Jim Taylor in the neighboring town of Clinton. Called on to surrender, they resisted, fought back, and all three died without having caused any damage to the posse members.[11] With Jim Taylor dead, John Wesley Hardin hiding out in far off Florida with his brother-in-law, also wanted on a murder charge, Bill Taylor was now the most wanted man in Texas.

Details of the next incident bringing sorrow to the Taylor family are few. Bill Taylor was charged with the killing of a black man.

The sole newspaper account citing this incident identified the victim as Willis Frier.[12] This supposedly happened in 1876; if the account is correct then he was wanted for two killings: that of Sutton and that of Frier. Now Bill Taylor wisely left the area and headed west, but on April 15, 1877, in Coleman County, Texas, Lt. B. S. Foster of Company E of the Texas Rangers caught up with him.[13] Coleman County is some eighty miles from DeWitt County. Obviously, Bill Taylor ought to have headed further west quicker than he did. He was allowed bail of $5000 "to await the action of the district court." Commented the *Victoria Advocate*, "The case will doubtless be a hard one for Billy."[14]

Bill Taylor must have had good lawyers defending him against the murder charge, as he was found not guilty, thus saving his neck from the noose. Apparently Taylor could not avoid trouble, as in early January of 1880, according to one report, "Bill Taylor again undertook to act at defiance the law of the land, and in company with several other young men, visited the home of a peaceable colored man, and after acts of violence drove Caesar Brown from his humble cabin, and ended the wrong by outraging the young daughter of that colored man."[15]

Taylor and one other, Charles Middleton, were arrested and jailed. This was in January. When R. H. Foster, with the responsibility of taking an accurate census of the county, visited the county jail in Cuero on June 17, 1880, he found one of the prisoners was William R. Taylor, his regular occupation given as "laborer." Prisoner Taylor was listed as twenty-five-years-old.[16]

This is the last known record of William Riley Taylor's presence in Texas. What became of him? Having avoided the hangman's noose for the Slaughter killing, and the Frier killing, seemingly able to avoid long stretches in a county jail, Taylor must have been cleared of the rape charge and now left the country.

By chance, although some might argue that chance had anything to do with it, the existence of an affidavit in the Kimble County, Texas, courthouse, located in Junction, was brought to this writer's attention. On May June 29, 1916, two men appeared before Notary Public Coke Stevenson, identified as W. W. Taylor and T. J. Bailey, "each known to me to be a credible person", swore to what amounted to a Taylor family tree. It stated, in brief, that Elizabeth Taylor never remarried after the loss of her husband, that she had died in 1886, that during her married life to William Taylor there were born nine children to the union: Creed Taylor, John M. Taylor, Joseph Taylor, W.P. Taylor, Martha Ann Taylor, Amanda Taylor, Jane Taylor, Delaney Taylor and Elizabeth Taylor. Creed Taylor had died on July 30, 1855, leaving only two children: J. Creed Taylor and William Taylor, "and William Taylor was killed in Oklahoma in the year 1895, and had never married and left his only heir, his brother, J. Creed Taylor."[17] This one line could be the solution to the mystery of what happened to the Texas fugitive Bill Taylor! But that is so incomplete, as every historian, amateur or professional, would demand to know the details of how this William Taylor was killed in Oklahoma in the year of 1895.

Knowing Taylor's past, one would not be surprised to learn that he was killed by an avenging relative of one of his victims from the days of the DeWitt County feud. Feudists have long memories. But being killed does not necessarily mean shot down in a gunfight. He may have accidentally shot himself while cleaning an "empty" pistol; or he may have been killed when his horse stumbled and fell on him. Life could end for this Texas gunfighter and feudist by any of numerous other possibilities. It would seem that he did not pass to his just reward from a disease, or some other manner of death, such as drowning, or being struck by lightning. Being "killed" suggests at the hand of someone else.

But this affidavit makes it clear that Bill Taylor, cousin of Jim Taylor, and the man who killed Gabe Slaughter on the deck of the steamer, *Clinton*, did pass in his chips somewhere in Oklahoma in 1895. Hopefully an astute member of WWHA can provide a more definite closure to the life of this man, William Riley "Bill" Taylor.

Chapter Twenty-One
The Search for A. R. Hendricks

By Chuck Parsons

Some individuals in Wild West History remain not much more than a name in our research files. Such a man is known only as A. R. Hendricks whose sole significance possibly is that he was inclined to be a fighting man instead of a passive observer; he was in the Confederate Army, a member of Captain L. H. McNelly's Texas Ranger militia, and then a member of the Taylor clan in the final days of the Sutton-Taylor Feud. He survived the army, survived the rangers but didn't survive the Taylor side during the feud. He left behind friends as well as a widow of three months.

Although we know almost nothing of his early life, we know certain important details of his death. He was shot to death December 27, 1875, on the streets of Clinton, Texas, with his two companions — James Creed Taylor and Mason "Winchester Smith" Arnold, by a posse composed of Sutton sympathizers. The three were taken across the Guadalupe River just outside Cuero and buried in what is today known as the Taylor-Bennett Cemetery. He has today a red granite headstone, a replacement of the small wooden markers.

Ironically, he received some recognition as early as 1880 when Victor M. Rose published the first study of the conflict entitled *The Texas Vendetta; or, The Sutton-Taylor Feud.* It was first published by the firm of J. J. Little of New York; then Ed Bartholomew, Texas historian, provided a facsimile of the book in 1956. This is what Victor M. Rose had to say of the final days of the feud: "Jim Taylor, one of the murderers of Sutton, was surrounded near Clinton by the Sutton clan, and, together with Mr. Hendricks and another of his partisans, killed."[53]

Not much to go on but significantly Rose addressed the man as

Mr. Hendricks instead of merely identifying him as a Taylor
feudist. The special sign of respect is noticeable.

Through the years of re-
search and writing about the
Wild West I have frequently
pondered this man, A. R. Hendricks. During the early years
while researching the life of
Captain McNelly, I "discovered" the name of Hendricks on
the muster rolls of McNelly. No
basic information was provided
about him, no state or county of
origin given as was provided
for some rangers on the muster
rolls. The one muster roll which
contains his name merely gives
rank and dates: he was mustered in as a sergeant on July 25,
1874, and served until February 24, 1875, earning an impressive
total payment of $224 for seven months.

James Creed "Jim" Taylor, leader of the
Taylor clan after the death of his father.
Chuck Parsons collection.

Fortunately, friends provided additional information, although
far less than hoped for. Edward J. Lanham, a Georgian who has a
great interest in Texas characters, informed me that the man I was
searching for was *Augustus R. Hendricks*. This man enlisted December 1, 1861, as a private in the 2nd Brush Battalion Cavalry. Not
surprisingly his service during the war enabled him to later enlist
as a sergeant in McNelly's militia.

In addition, researcher Tom Todd of Colorado, provided additional assistance. Todd provided information that A. R. Hendricks
enlisted in the Confederate States Army August 14, 1862, at Green-
ville, Texas, in Company A, 2nd Texas Infantry, for the duration of
the war. He was taken a prisoner of war, but was paroled at Vicks-
burg, Mississippi, on July 7, 1863. He did not return to his unit and
was considered a deserter. There the record ends until he enlisted
in McNelly's Washington County Militia Company of Texas Rang-

ers. These are differing documents but not necessarily conflicting documents. The statement which all sources agree is that he did serve as a soldier. Until he enlisted in McNelly's company in 1874 his life remains a blank.

After mustering his company, McNelly went to DeWitt County to attempt settling the two factions from creating unrest which affected the citizens. McNelly wrote to Adjutant General William Steele the progress of his duty:

> On arrival here about the 1st of Aug[us]t, a perfect reign of terror existed in this and adjoining counties; armed bands of men were making predatory excursions throughout the country, overawing the law-abiding citizens, while the civil authorities were unable, or unwilling to enforce the law framed for their protection. The lives of peaceable citizens who had given no cause of offence to either party were in jeopardy, as neutrals were considered obnoxious to both factions. From the facility with which treaties of peace had been broken, confidence in each other's respective promises was a thing unknown. In a country of such strong prejudices much has been accomplished by the good conduct of the state troops which has been most exemplary. No sympathy with, or favoritism to, either party has been shown by the men of this command, and our presence here is looked on by all peaceful citizens and is considered by them to be an absolute necessity for their protection and for the welfare of the country. Many men whose lives have hitherto been insecure, have been enabled to attend to their usual avocations in peace, although boasts have been made that our withdrawal will be the signal for a renewal of hostilities.

This shows conclusively that McNelly and his troops did do some good in DeWitt County during the feud. Although no battles were fought, Sergeant A. R. Hendricks did perform some work which was above and beyond his duty as a McNelly man.

Perhaps at one of the dances held in Cuero or Clinton he met a member of the fairer sex, Elizabeth Jane Day, as she was born, but through the years she tragically lost husbands: her first husband — Joseph W. Bennett, was believed killed by Indians; her second — George W. Rivers, deserted during the war; her third husband —William B. Kelly, was killed by members of the Sutton force leaving her a widow again.

Somehow the widow Bennett-Rivers-Kelly met and gave in to the charms of A. R. Hendricks. He had resigned from the ranger force in February 1875; he and Elizabeth Kelly were joined in matrimony in Lafayette County, Texas, on September 23, 1875.

As a man married to the widow of a man who lost his life to a Sutton posse — what could he plan for the remainder of his life? The couple could have left the country as Bill Sutton had planned to do in March of 1874, but lost his life to Jim Taylor in a gunfight.

After all, she had her children to care for: William Edwin Bennett, Joseph Bennett, Susan Rivers and M. L. "Willis" Kelly, daughter of William B. Kelly killed by the Sutton posse.

Census enumerator, Willis Fawcett, had found the Kelly family in household number 214 while doing the census in 1870; next door in number 215 was the home of Pitkin Barnes Taylor, with wife, Susan, and two children: James and Mary, nineteen and sixteen respectively.

Elizabeth perhaps had too many friends and acquaintances in DeWitt County to leave, and maybe they both believed the feud was coming to an end. It was not.

No doubt being the husband of Elizabeth Kelly (née Day) he met many members of the Kelly family: Jack Hays Day, Alford Creed Day and certainly his wife's half-brother, James Creed Taylor. Having been one of McNelly's rangers he certainly recalled that at one point the captain resolved to capture Jim Taylor and Wes Hardin or kill his horses running them to earth. He failed to do either, but certainly tried hard enough.

Before he could accomplish his DeWitt County goals, Adj. Gen. Steele ordered McNelly and his company of state troops to the Rio Grande frontier in an effort to halt the huge amount of cattle stealing done by raiders from across the river. If Hendricks had remained a single man, he would no doubt have gone to the Rio Grande frontier and lived to tell the tale.

But Hendricks remained in DeWitt County and developed a friendship with his wife's half-brother, Jim Taylor. Another young man who by joining them formed a triumvirate of feudists was

Mason "Winchester Smith" Arnold, apparently a one-time resident of Schulenberg, Lavaca County, Texas, but now in DeWitt to remove himself from his troubles there.

According to Taylor family lore, Jim Taylor felt that if he would stand trial with a good lawyer to defend him, he would be acquitted of the Sutton killing. For this reason, he and his two friends —Arnold and Hendricks, were in Clinton that day of December 27, 1875. Before they could make any contact with an attorney — T. T. Teel, members of the Sutton force learned they were in town, and thus were available for arrest or killing.

According to Jack Hays Day, the trio was in Clinton to meet with attorney Teel. Day of course provided a version quite different than the accounts left

The elaborate headstone of Jim Taylor with the crossed Winchester rifles on top. The inscription provides his birth date as born January 15, 1851and the death date incorrectly as January 1, 1875, with the lines "An amiable father here lies at rest; / As ever God with his image blest,/ The friend of man, the friend of truth,/ The friend of age, the guide of youth." *Chuck Parsons collection*

by Sutton's sympathizers — that the three were in town to burn the courthouse down to destroy any indictments against them and their friends.

No contemporary source mentions attorney Teel having an interest in the feud at this point and Day's version is perhaps as much folklore as the idea of burning the courthouse. What is accepted as fact is that they stabled their horses in the livery owned by Martin V. King.

What happened next is controversial. From available contemporary sources, Richard B. Hudson, a strong supporter of the Suttons acting as a deputy under Sheriff William J. Weisiger who replaced the late Jack Helm. Hendricks, Taylor and Arnold apparently met up with several others who may have been friends or merely acquaintances — Tom King, son of Martin V. King; and Ed Davis. While this group was acting together, Hudson was gathering another group to deal with Jim Taylor specifically. After all, he had a reward on his head, courtesy the widow Sutton.

Hudson had gathered what he termed a posse of Sutton sympathizers: Christopher T. "Kit" Hunter, "Curry" Wallace, Bill Meador, Buck McCrabb, John McCrabb, Frank Cox, Bill Cox, Jake Ryan and brothers, Joe and Ed Sitterle. If proved to be a tough group to go against Jim Taylor and two friends.

Similar to the action at the so-called "Gunfight at the O.K. Corral" of Tombstone, no one can say who fired the first shot of the engagement. These men, deputized by Sheriff Weisiger, were informed that Tom King and Ed Davis were not to be harmed as the sheriff had made a deal with Martin King to lock the stable, denying access to the horses.

The result was that Kit Hunter, firing his Winchester, managed to shoot Jim Taylor in the right arm, breaking it, causing him to drop his weapon. Jim Taylor had been aiming at Hunter but only put a bullet through his hat. The others proved to be an effective fighting force and within moments Taylor, Hendricks and Arnold were dead or wounded. A number of newspaper reports are available but perhaps the most complete is that of the *Galveston Daily News* published in its issue of January 1, 1876. It is here printed in full, the reporter identified only as "Reliable Source."

> Since Sunday night [December 26] Jim Taylor, with two or three men, have been in and around Clinton, walking through the streets with two six-shooters on each; and, as our sheriff was at home and remained there, no arrest was made. The party had, in conversation with Martin King, sent Dick Hudson word that they would come and kill him unless he left the county within 24 hours.
>
> Dick could not exactly see the point, and together with six or seven of the Sutton boys, went to Clinton Monday, Dec. 27th, to offer his service to the Sheriff. As they reached there and dismounted, the Taylors (five men) at once got their guns [Winchesters], and commenced

A view of the Taylor-Bennett Cemetery before being cleaned. The view shows Jim Taylor's tall imposing headstone and to the left the now replaced with a granite stone the graves of Arnold and Hendricks. To the right of Jim Taylor's stone is that of his father and mother, Pitkin B. and Susan Taylor. *Chuck Parsons collection.*

firing and retreating through a field, the Sutton party after them, and after hard running and much shooting, Jim Taylor, Winchester Smith [Mace Arnold], (the man who is now recognized as having given Rup [*sic*, Rube] Brown the first shot when he was killed,) and Hendricks (one of Capt. McNelly's command, who married into the Taylor family) were killed. Mark [*sic*] King and young Toggles [*sic*, Tuggle] threw up their hands and surrendered, and were, therefore, not hurt.

According to the memoirs of Daniel Fore Chisholm, an obvious sympathizer of the Taylors, claims that when the shooting stopped, the posse "rode in a wide circle around Jim Taylor and Mace Arnold, until they were sure they were both dead. Then they rode up to them and one of the gang used a double-barreled shotgun loaded with buckshot and shot one side of Mace Arnold's face and head off."

Also, Chisholm remembered that the dying Hendricks was still alive and asked Bill Meador if he could go see his wife for the last time. Meador volunteered the use of his own horse. But before

Hendricks got very far, "the rest of the gang" met him. Dick Hudson asked of the group who would "finish Hendricks off" and Kit Hunter volunteered. He "put his gun against Hendricks' ear and pulled the trigger."

All that followed was the burial of the three men in what is now the Taylor-Bennett Cemetery. One other act was necessary: the trial of the members of the posse which killed the three men; it may have been a mere formality. The Grand Jury met on April 3, 1876, and found that R. B. Hudson, J. R. McCrabb, William Cox, Jeff White, Henry White, W. C. Wallace, John Meador, William Meador and Christopher T. Hunter were charged with murder. Ultimately the charges were dropped; the men who killed Hendricks, Taylor and Arnold were free to go and the district attorney removed the indictments from the docket.

By marrying into the Taylor family, A. R. Hendricks added one more sorrow in the life of his widow. Elizabeth Jane Hendricks, now faced with the task of burying her fourth husband, certainly realized how dearly the feud had cost her.

Chapter Twenty-Two
Wild West Interrogatives

Note: Interviews connected to the release of Parsons' and Brown's biography on John Wesley Hardin in 2013.

Two questions were asked concerning John Wesley Hardin.

1. "Is there any truth to the story that John Wesley Hardin shot a man for snoring? If so, when and where did this happen — if not, how did the story get started?"

Hardin wrote in his autobiography, first published in 1896, after his death, describing his experience in Abilene, Kansas, in 1871, "In those days my life was constantly in danger from secret or hired assassins, and I was always on the lookout."

He does not explain who these "secret or hired assassins" would be, and one wonders why there would be any in Kansas anyway. To the vast majority of people, in 1871, in Kansas, Hardin was just another cowboy who had driven cattle up the trail from Texas.

In Abilene, in the American House hotel, he did kill a man. He described the killing in dramatic terms, which contrast strongly with how the contemporary press described the killing. The *Abilene Chronicle* reported it within days; Hardin wrote of it more than twenty years after the fact. According to Hardin, he and his cousin, John Gibson "Gip" Clements, were staying in the American House and one night: "I heard a man cautiously unlock my door and slip in with a dirk in his hand. I halted him with a shot and he ran; I fired at him again and again, and he fell dead with four bullets in his body."

Then he and Clements left Abilene for good, heading home for Texas. This is Hardin's version of his last killing in Kansas.

We can be thankful for the existence of the local weekly newspaper, the *Abilene Chronicle*. In the issue of August 10, 1871, was a report that the killing occurred the night of August 6 in the American House. The victim's name was Charles Couger. The *Chronicle* reported:

> A most fiendish murder was perpetrated at the American House . . . Couger was a boss cattle herder, and said to be a gentleman. Couger was in his room sitting upon the bed reading a newspaper. Four shots were fired at him, through a board partition, one of which struck him in the fleshy part of the left arm, passing through the third rib and entering the heart, cutting a piece of it entirely off, and killing Couger almost instantly. The murderer escaped his pursuers. If caught he will probably be killed on sight.

In neighboring town Salina, the *Salina Weekly Journal* added to the report, stating that the man was killed "by a desperado called 'Arkansas.' The murderer fled. This was his sixth murder [in Kansas]." This appeared in the issue of August 10, 1871.

So, Couger was shot and killed while sitting on a bed reading a newspaper. But what probably happened was Couger sat down to read the paper, fell asleep, and began to snore. Hardin and Clements probably were unable to sleep themselves, so Hardin fired his pistol a few times toward the snoring man, and by chance killed him. When the coroner found him, he was on the bed, the paper probably partially covering his corpse.

Back in Texas how did Hardin and Clements explain their adventures in Kansas? We don't know the details but certainly the subject of the killing in the American House came up. By then it may have become a "Wes killed a man for snoring" tale.

Of great interest is that after Hardin's capture in 1877 and being incarcerated in the Travis County jail, he was interviewed by a reporter, probably from the *Statesman* newspaper. Thomas E. Hogg wrote a book about dealing with the Sam Bass gang and included a conversation held between the reporter and Hardin. This supposedly occurred in 1878 while Hardin was waiting to be returned to Comanche for sentencing.

Hardin was described as being "pert and saucy" as ever and was quoted as saying, "They tell lots of lies about me. They say I killed six or seven men for snoring, but it isn't true. I only killed one man for snoring."

This suggests that Hardin was very much aware of what had really happened in the American House back in 1871 and treated it almost as a joke. [Thomas E. Hogg wrote this up in his book *The Life and Adventures of Sam Bass The Notorious Union Pacific and Texas Train Robber* published in 1878, pages 68-69.]

So, the story of the "snoring man" — Charles Couger — getting killed for snoring is at least in part true. Hardin did not shoot him intending to kill him for snoring; he no doubt intended for his four shots to disturb him enough so he would stop snoring. Of interest is that Hardin recalled shooting *four shots* to cause the snoring to cease; the *Chronicle* reported four shots as well. Interesting!

2. "It is said that Hardin studied law while in prison, passed the Texas bar and became an attorney. What kind of education did he have in his youth that would give him the ability to accomplish this? And what quality of lawyer did he make? Are there any records available that would give some insight into his new-found career?"

First of all, we have a great deal of material written by John Wesley Hardin before his prison years, during his prison years, and some following. There is more material written by him than perhaps any other gunfighter of the Wild West. He was the son of a minister, thus his education was certainly better than the average young person in the 1850s and 1860s.

This cannot be proven certainly, but it stands to reason that the family did teach some reading abilities by studying the *Bible*. We know from his autobiography as well and by several contemporary sources that he was hired to do some school teaching; if a school board decided he could act as a classroom teacher in the mid to late 1860s he must have had an above average ability with the basics. His teaching was perhaps not much more than basic math and basic reading and basic penmanship.

There is a huge collection of his letters housed today at Texas State University in San Marcos, Texas. I have read the originals as well as the letters transcribed in the book by the Stamps, [*The Letters of John Wesley Hardin* transcribed by Roy and Jo Ann Stamps.] His letters are not difficult to read — other than the fact that frequently he had limited paper and thus wrote quite small — and the occasional misspelled word and less than perfect grammar.

During his sixteen plus years in prison he read, as well as wrote letters preserved by his family, and in so doing, improved his reading and writing as well as thinking beyond the present. He certainly — as an outlaw — learned various aspects of the law — as one in flight. He knew enough about law and order to claim that if he were guaranteed a fair trial, he would surrender and stand trial. But of course while he was a free man anyone wanting to arrest him became a vigilante only wanting to harm his body and deny him his freedom, hence he never surrendered. And he had to kill to defend himself from these would be assassins and men wanting to take his freedom.

During his prison years he considered the profession of law. And he did stand a bar exam, although by today's standards it would be considered nothing more than a near-meaningless quiz on the subject. The *Gonzales Inquirer* reported in its issue of July 26, 1894:

> Mr. John Wesley Hardin was examined by a committee of the Gonzales bar this week and having passed a suitable examination in the principles of law, was granted a license by the court to practice in the district court and all inferior courts.

The examining committee was composed of C. A. Burchard, W.W. Glass, B.R. Abernathy and H.A. Nixon. Judge T. H. Spooner of the 25th Judicial District was in charge. With license in hand, he opened up an office in the newly erected Peck & Fly Building in Gonzales, a building which still stands today overlooking the Confederate Square in the county seat's downtown section.

Was he an excellent attorney? No. He had few clients, and he had no big cases. He was added to the prosecution team when James Brown Miller was prosecuting George Frazer, but Hardin was added probably because of his relationship to Miller, not that Miller had such high confidence in him.

There are a few documents concerning his legal matters in the Hardin Collection at Texas State University, but I doubt if there are enough for anyone to come to any conclusions on his talent as a lawyer.

* * *

Lewis Nordyke, Richard Marohn and Leon C. Metz wrote
biographies of Hardin. Thus one might understandably wonder
why we would write another one. Here is a possible explanation.
First, Norm Brown:

> A number of years ago I learned that John Wesley Har-
> din's brother, Jeff, was killed in a gunfight in 1901. The
> killing took place about thirty miles, as the crow flies,
> from my home. The town of Clairemont was never very
> big and when the railroad missed it, the town dried up
> and died. Then, I started researching the other brothers
> of John Wesley and discovered Gip Hardin had killed
> a deputy sheriff that sent him to prison in Huntsville,
> an incident which indicated Gip had followed in big
> brother's footsteps. Of course, I knew that Joe, the old-
> est, had been lynched back in 1874 so it was my think-
> ing that at least three of Reverend J. G. Hardin's sons
> died violently.
>
> My interest in the Hardin family somehow caught the
> attention of Chuck Parsons and we discovered our in-
> terests were basically the same which was to take a very
> close look at these Hardins and do our best to write an
> accurate and complete biography of one of the quickest
> and deadliest gunfighters of the Wild West.

Parsons adds:

> We think we have done that; we discovered new in-
> formation; we determined some of the stories about
> the Hardin's were not true; we found some were only
> half true; we determined some of the killings he wrote
> about happened, but not quite the way he described
> them. And of course, there were some which he forgot
> about — or ignored — when writing his autobiogra-
> phy. If all goes according to plan the book will be avail-
> able in early 2013. [It was published in 2013 by UNT
> Press, Denton.] We are planning on traveling to Boise
> this coming summer to attend the WWHA Roundup to
> help promote the book, entitled *A Lawless Breed: John*

Wesley Hardin, Texas Reconstruction, and Violence in the Wild West." Published by the University of North Texas Press, it will be in excess of 500 pages, have around eighty illustrations — some of which have never been published — and have a foreword by Leon C. Metz.

We do not claim that our work will be better than the writings of Nordyke, Marohn and Metz, as they were important to us in our research. We do feel, however, that we found enough new material and interpretations to make *A Lawless Breed: John Wesley Hardin, Texas Reconstruction and Violence in the Wild West* a worthy contribution to the Wild West genre.

Hopefully, this anthology *Bad Blood: The Violent Lives of John Welsey Hardin, of the Hardin Brothers and Some Associates* brings new discoveries in correcting history and filling in those blank spaces. Descendants like Diann Webb, who has the *Bible* records of Deputy Charles Webb's family and another descendant who knew that Gip Hardin did not die at sea were priceless. Finding the answers from long ago is difficult, no doubt. With luck, we will continue to learn more of the Old West and its notorious and colorful characters.

Reverend Hardin Letter to Bell

Dodds City Nov. 10, 1895
Dear Bell—

I am here just starting home for Red River County. I have been attending court at Bonham. One of my mules died with the blind staggers while here. We are always glad to hear from you and the sweet little ones. God bless you and them. My address is Paris, Lamar County. We have a good home but hard run. We live twenty miles from Paris, near Denison Flys saw mill.

North of Starkville. We would be glad you could come and spend two or three months with us or as long as you could. The cars run in nine miles of Paris to Brookston. You could come there on the cars and get a hack to drive you out. All want to see you. Write soon. My love to Bint Cobb and his. Excuse this hurried letter. My Br. Robert from Bonham was up to see me. Jeff and Vannie are here with me. Sweet peace to you. J.W.S. Hardin

Appendix B

John Wesley Hardin Assault Crime

THE STATE OF TEXAS,

County of Navarro

In the District Court of said county,

October Term, A. D. 1870

In and by the Authority of the State of Texas,

The Grand Jurors, good and lawful men of the State of Texas, County of Navarro duly tried on Oath by the Judge of the District Court of said County, touching their legal qualifications as Grand Jurors, elected, empanneled, sworn and charged to inquire into and true presentments make of all offences against the penal laws of said State, committed within the body of the County aforesaid, upon their Oaths present in the District Court of said County; That John Hardin

late of the County of Navarro Laborer, on the 26th day of August in the year of our Lord one thousand eight hundred and ~~seventy~~ Sixty nine with force and arms in the County of Navarro and State of Texas, did then and there with a certain six shooting pistol did then and there in and upon the body of one S H Presley wilfully feloniously and of his malice aforethought did make an assault with the intent then and there him the said S H Presley wilfully feloniously and of his malice aforethought to kill and murder —

contrary to the form of the Statute in such cases made and provided, and against the peace and dignity of the State.

Dm Lockett

177

Appendix C
John Wesley Hardin Prison Record

From the Texas State Prison Archives for Huntsville Prison   803

Appendix D

Lizzie Bell Marries J. B. Cobb, Comanche, Texas

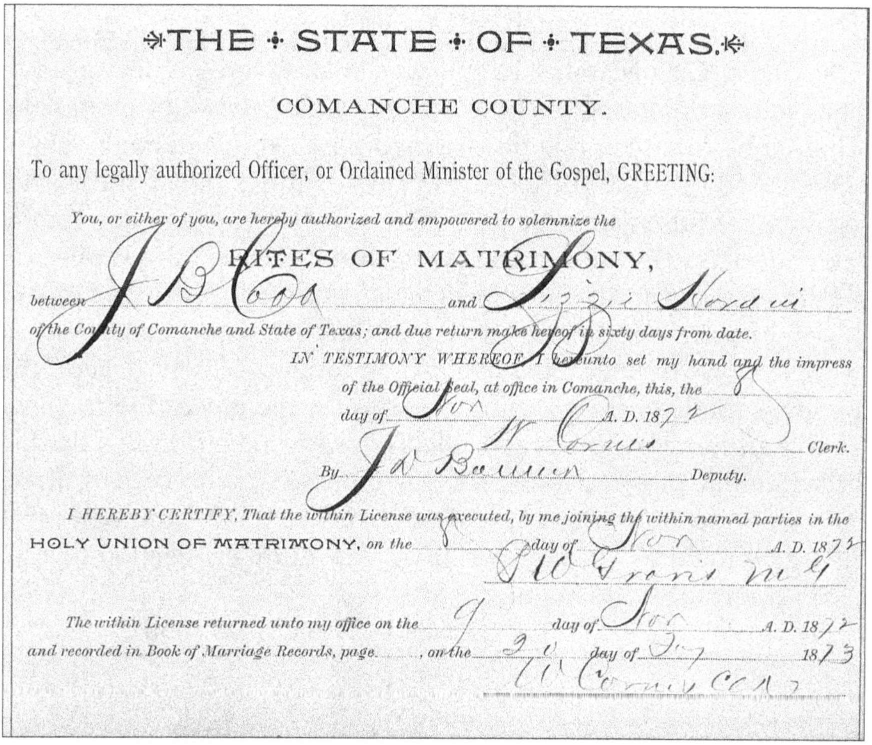

Appendix E
The Authentic Cuero Marshal Badge of R. H. Brown

The badge was contributed by Donald M. Yena.

The Cuero City Marshal badge was sold several years ago at a San Antonio, Texas, gun show by a Mr. Bob Ashby from Houston. The Ashby family at one time owned pawn shops in the Houston area and the badge turned up in one of those pawn shops. Records regarding it are now lost. Also, several years ago Bob Ashby (now deceased) sold this badge to a South Texas badge collector, dealer, and authority who in turn sold this badge to us, Donald M. and Louise Yena, for inclusion in their extensive collections of related Texas memorabilia. An "eagle topped" shield design, the badge is made of nickel using the double dye method with "jeweler" hand engraved enamel filled lettering. The findings (badge attachments, pins, catchers, etc.) are consistent with badges of the 1870s period of manufacture. In the future this badge will most likely be included in a major Texas museum's collection of rare and important Texas lawmen's artifacts.

— Donald M. Yena

Appendix F
Overview of Gip Hardin's Murder Trial

March 28, 1898 — (Monday night) This was the end of the watch for Deputy Sheriff John Turman, Kimble County Sheriff's Office.

March 29, 1898 — Gip Hardin-Case number 657 — Charged with Murder-Entered plea "not guilty"-Court sets trial date for April 4.

March 29, 1898 — Murder trial of A. W. Haley, case number 653, change of venue from Sutton County, officially postponed as both his and Hardin's trail dates set for April 4. Judge Wm. Allison of the 33rd Judicial District ordered Haley's case be continued and ordered Hardin's case to be heard April 4.

March 31, 1898 — Hardin obtains legal counsel and given until April 4, 1898 to prepare for trial.

April 4, 1898 — Gip Hardin's defense makes a motion to squash the murder charge. The motion was denied. He requested a change of venue for the trial and that motion also denied.

April 5, 1898 — Defense requested a continuance and that was denied. Then, it seemed all attempts for a fair trial were falling apart. Gip entered his not guilty plea again on that date. J. W. Wilson is selected as foreman of the jury and eleven other men are picked to serve as jurors. The trial begins.

April 8, 1898 — Jury left the box to deliberate a verdict. They quickly made a decision and returned to the courtroom and the Judge asked the foreman, Mr. Wilson, if a verdict had been reached. He answered in the affirmative and stated that the jury found the defendant Gip Hardin, guilty of murder in the second degree. The clerk was instructed to read the verdict back to the court, which he did. Then, the judge polled the jurors and they all affirmed the guilty finding. The Judge then sentenced Hardin to thirty-five years state prison. Gip then requested an appeal for a new trial and was given ten days to prepare and file a statement of facts.

April 9, 1898 — Judge Addison asked Gip Hardin if he wished to make a statement and he declined. The Judge then stated that the sentence of thirty-five years imprisonment would be stayed while the court awaited the decision of the Criminal Appeals Court to determine if the verdict and the sentence would be upheld. He then stated that Gip Hardin would remain in County jail while awaiting the decision of the higher court. The Judge then affirmed that the Jurors would be paid $2 per day for their service and the sheriff would receive $26.

February 15, 1899 — Texas State Court of Criminal Appeals. The verdict was overturned and the court was ordered to reverse the conviction of murder and the prison sentence and further instructed the 33rd District court to transfer Gip Hardin to Gillespie County prior to the September 1899 term for said county.

"The sheriff is hereby instructed to transfer Gip Hardin to Gillespie County jail prior to the September, 1899", ordered Judge Wm. Addison.

Appendix G
Jo Hardin False Letter From Dixson

Chappell Hill Texas December
27th AD 1872
Received of Jo.G. Hardin, my agent t[o]
Sell the Solomon Grubler 320 acres of
Land in Comanche County State of
Texas, two hundred & Eighty two Dollars $282.00
receipt in full for all demands against
my said Agent & I hereby acknowledge
full payment for said tract of which
my said Agent sold for me
                                    G J Dixon

Inside Cover of Jeff Hardin Stable Ledger

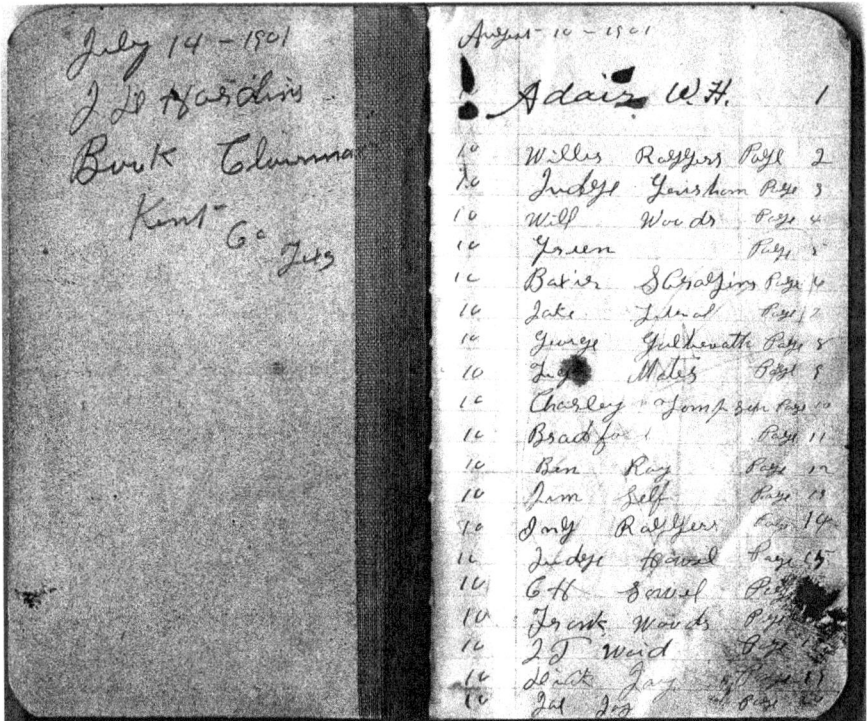

Endnotes

Chapter One

1. Hardin, Jefferson D., Grandson of Jefferson Davis Hardin, email conversations about his family history, Feb., 2017.

2. Atnip, Ronnie, Fannin County historian, information obtained during an interview circa 2015.

3. *Ibid.*

Chapter Two

1. Disregard the belief that William Webb was Charles Webb's father. New information from bible records and Descendent Dianne Webb clarifies the family linage. See chapter five for a better accounting.

Chapter Three

1. Parsons, Chuck and Brown, Norman Wayne, *A Lawless Breed, John Wesley Hardin, Texas Reconstruction, and Violence In The Wild West*, Denton, TX; University of North Texas Press, 2013.

2. Teagarden, W. B., letter dated November 2nd, 1931, to Mrs. Charles Billings, Nopal, TX.

3. William Baker Teagarden (1854-1933). He was an attorney, judge and representative of the Southern Pacific Railroad for many years.

4. Feinstein, Sherman C., Editor, *Annals of the American Society for Adolescent Psychiatry, Developmental and Clinical Studies*, Volume 14, Chicago, IL, University of Chicago Press, 1987.

Chapter Four

1. Barry A. Crouch and Donaly E. Brice. *The Governor's Hounds: The Texas State Police, 1870 -1873.* (Austin: University of Texas Press. 2011).

2. John Wesley Hardin. *The Life of John Wesley Hardin, as Written by Himself*, 61-62. First published by Smith & Moore of Seguin, Texas in 1896. For this paper I have used the University of Oklahoma Press reprint of 1961 with an introduction by Robert G. McCubbin. Hereafter referred to as Hardin, *Life.*

3. John Wesley Hardin to his wife Jane Bowen Hardin, June 24, 1888. The Hardin letters are preserved as The John Wesley Hardin Collection, The Wittliff Collection, Texas State University, San Marcos, Texas.

4. For excellent studies of these two men see *Cullen Montgomery Baker: Reconstruction Desperado* by Barry A. Crouch and Donaly E. Brice (Baton Rouge, LA: Louisiana State University Press, 1997) and *Bloody Bill Longley: The Mythology of a Gunfighter* by Rick Miller (Denton: University of North Texas Press, 2011).

5. *Flake's Daily Bulletin*, February 4, 1871, reprinting item from the *Fairfield Ledger* of January 28, 1871.

6. Crouch and Brice. *The Governor's Hounds*, 291.

7. Hardin, *Life*, 32-33.

8. *Ibid.*, 62

9. The spelling of this man's name varies as to source. For consistency I have used the spelling which appears in Governor Davis's reward proclamation. According to the Gonzales County Census of 1870 Green Parramore was a black laborer, thirty-five-years-old and born in Georgia. He claimed $100 personal estate and no real estate. His family consisted of Lucinda, thirty and black, born in Mississippi; children daughter Corly, fourteen and Rena, three and son James, two months of age. None in the household could read or write. Their post office was Belmont in precinct #3. Enumerated by M.H. Beaty, 471.

10. According to the Gonzales County Census of 1870 mulatto John Lackey was a thirty-three-

year-old blacksmith, born in Tennessee with a personal estate of $600. His wife Eliza was a twenty-eight-year-old Indian from Arkansas. Their five children, all identified as mulattos, were ten-year-old Fannie, John, eleven, twins Florence and Charles, seven, and Dennis, five. From the census the Lackeys lived in Arkansas until 1860 and then located in Texas. Also in the household was an eighteen-year-old mulatto born in Missouri, working as an apprentice to blacksmith Lackey. Enumerated by M.H. Beaty, 406.

11. Hardin, *Life*, 62-63.

12. Proclamation of Rewards

13. Hardin, *Life*, 63.

14. *San Antonio Herald* in an undated issue and then reprinted in *Flake's Semi-Weekly Bulletin*, October 18, 1871.

15. Hardin, *Life*, 64.

16. Ledger of Letters Received, 401.702 Texas State Archives, 89/

17. Sammy Tise. *Texas County Sheriffs*, privately printed, 1989, 446.

18. 1860 Milam County Census, 17. The census enumerator was William M. Speights, the father of J.H.H. Speights.

19. Hardin, *Life*, 67.

20. Crouch and Brice, *The Governor's Hounds*, 165.

21. The first Adjutant General, James Davidson, disappeared from Texas history when ostensibly on a business trip to New York he chose to continue his journey to Canada and then to Europe where he ultimately settled in New Zealand. Thus Frank L. Britton became the new Adjutant General.

22. Frank L. Britton. *Report of the Adjutant General, of the State of Texas ,for the Year 1872.* (Austin: James P. Newcomb and Company, 1872), 12..

23. *Ibid.*, 9.

24. *San Antonio Herald*, November 26, 1872, citing an undated *Lone Star Ranger*.

25. Sheriff W.E. Jones to Adjutant General, November 1, 1872. Summary of Letters Received, Ledger 401-620, 285.

26. *Ibid.*, November 20, 1872, 286.

27. Fannin County, Texas historian Ronnie Atnip.

Chapter Five

1. Webb, Dianna, direct descendant, her family bible, and the federal census records of 1850, 1860, and 1870.

2. Webb, Dianna, email communication. She also provided a copy of the Webb Bible record.

3. Unnamed member of Major W. M. Green's Texas Ex-Ranger Association. He wrote an article that appeared in *Frontier Times*, May, 1924 edition.

4. *The Houston Telegraph*, Houston, TX, June 3, 1874.

5. *Ibid.*

Chapter Six

1. James W. Mann was born in Santa Rosa County, Florida, although there are discrepancies in the census. He was the son of James W. and Mary Elizabeth Mann; in 1860 he is shown to be one-year-old. A decade later the family still resided in Santa Rosa County, but he is now shown to be fourteen- years-old, suggesting a birth year of 1856. Hardin wrote that when he was killed in August 1877, he was nineteen years of age which may be correct. Federal Census for Santa Rosa County, Florida, 1860 and 1870.

2. Sheppard Hardy appears in the Federal Census of 1870 in Santa Rosa County, Florida as a thirty-three-year-old laborer. Then he had a twenty-seven-year-old wife, Sarah. In 1880 he is in Baldwin County,

Alabama, still a laborer but now with eight children ranging in age from twenty-one years down to two years. All were born in Florida.

3. Neil Campbell Jr. was also a laborer, identified occupation being "logger" in the 1880 Santa Rosa County, Florida Census. In 1880 he is shown to be twenty-five-years-old, his wife Amazone, twenty-years-old, and a one-year-old son. Neil Campbell Jr. lived from 1854 to 1922. His wife lived from 1860 to 1935; her headstone identifies her as Anna Campbell. Apparently Campbell had no trouble with the law even though he was considered an associate of Hardin.

4. Hardin. *Life*, 117.

5. William Henry Hutchinson was born in Prattville, Autauga County, Alabama on June 7, 1845, the son of Thomas Walton and Ann Fralick Hutchinson, but was raised in the neighborhood of Montgomery, Alabama. On March 6, 1862 he enlisted in Company K of the 1st Alabama Regiment in Prattville for three years. By 1864 he was secret scout under General J.H. Clanton but was captured at Port Hudson on July 9, 1863. At war's end he returned home where he worked in his father's store. In 1868 the family moved to Pensacola and opened a mercantile store on South Palafax Street. He married Miss Alice Stanley McKenzie on October 1, 1868 and ran for sheriff of Escambia County in 1876. After his first wife's death he married Ila Temple Merritt. Hutchinson died on January 14, 1911. Hutchinson's Application for Pension # 3695; Widow's Application for Pension; obituaries from the *Pensacola Journal*, January 15, 1911, and *Pensacola News*, January 14, 1911; unpublished biographical sketch by Lola Lee Daniell Bruington. Copy in author's possession.

6. Leon Metz expressed it best in his *John Wesley Hardin: Dark Angel of Texas* (El Paso: Mangan Books, 1996): "Sheriff Hutchinson, nonchalantly strolled through, throwing off drunks and undesirables while mentally evaluating Hardin and his friends."168.

7. This man remains somewhat of a mystery figure. He is perhaps the Alexander John Perdue, born in New York in 1815. The 1850 Mobile County, Alabama, census shows him as a thirty-five-year-old carpenter. It is believed he is the same man who died on July 21, 1892 at Warrington, Escambia County, Florida. Florida Death Index, 1877-1998, vol. 2 # 928 and Federal Census Mobile County, Alabama 1850.

8. Sources do not agree on how the quartet was seated. On the news of Hardin's death in 1895 Jack Duncan granted a lengthy interview in which he stated Hardin was seated in a seat by himself and Mann was in the seat ahead of him. *Galveston Daily News*, August 23, 1895.

9. Hardin. *Life*, 117.

10. *Montgomery Daily Advertiser and Mail*, August 28, 1877.

11. Hardin. *Life*, 118. The latter version is from the *Austin Daily Democratic Statesman*, August 29, 1877.

12. Telegram from Lt. J.B. Armstrong to Adj. Gen. William Steele, August 25, 1877.

13. Allen Marion McMillan was the son of Malcom and Mary Jane McCaskill McMillan, born March 28, 1843. By 1880 he was probate judge of Escambia County, Alabama. He died May 31, 1896. Federal Census of Escambia County, Alabama 1880, 235; and Cemetery Inventory of Coon Hill Cemetery, Santa Rosa County, Florida.

14. "J.H. Swain" to Jane, August 25, 1877.

15. *Denison (Texas) Daily News*, August 26, 1877. Reprint from the *Dallas Daily Commercial*.

16. Hardin. *Life*, 121.

17. *Galveston Daily News*, August 23, 1895.

18. *Montgomery Daily Advertiser and Mail*, August 28, 1877.

19. William Dudley Chipley, Information on William Dudley Chipley is from Edward C. Williamson's "William D. Chipley, Western Florida's Mr. Railroad." In *The Florida Historical Quarterly*, Vol. XXV, No. 4, April 1947.

20. *Austin Daily Democratic Statesman*, September 7, 1877, reprinting undated article from *Dallas Daily Herald*.

21. John E. Callaghan was a lumber merchant in Pensacola, 45-years-old with a wife and two children. Federal Census Escambia County, Florida, 1880.

22. *El Paso Daily Times*, September 8, 1895.

23. For full biographical treatments of Hutchinson and Duncan, see *The Capture of John Wesley Hardin* by Parsons, and *Bounty Hunter* by Rick Miller.

24. Alexander Sweet. *On A Mexican Mustang through Texas, From the Gulf to the Rio Grande* (Hartford, Conn.: S.S. Scranton & Co., 1883), 426-27.

25. *Pensacola Gazette*, Reprinted from the *Montgomery Advertiser and Mail*, August 26, 1877.

26. W.D. Chipley to Gov. R.B. Hubbard, August 28, 1877.

27. *Montgomery Daily Advertiser and Mail*, September 19, 1877.

28. *Ibid.*, October 28, 1877. Henry Sutton was no relation to the William E. Sutton of the Sutton-Taylor Feud notoriety.

Chapter Seven

1. John Selman's version of killing Hardin is from the *El Paso Herald*, August 20, 1895.

2. The statements from Selman, Brown, Shackelford and Anderson are all from the *El Paso Herald*, August 20, 1895.

3. Hubbard, "A Boy's Impression of El Paso in the 1890's." Hubbard recalled that if he received a telegram for Hardin in the morning he would take it to his room; if it was received in the afternoon he found Hardin in one of the several saloons he frequented. Hubbard, in the fall of 1899, entered as a freshman in the University of Texas. He later became president of Texas Woman's University in Denton. He died on July 13, 1973, and is buried in Oakwood Cemetery in Austin. His simple headstone shows only his full name and the dates of his life: 1882–1973.

4. From the scrapbook of Attorney Adrian D. Storms in the Special Collections, University of Texas-El Paso Library. This is a combination of drawings and notes and clippings from various El Paso newspapers.

5. *El Paso Daily Times*, August 21, 1895, in the popular column "Around Town." Commented the *Times*: "The city was as quiet as a country church yard last night. The police had nothing to do."

6. This assessment is based on author Brown's extensive military experiences of seeing head wounds from enemy fire.

Chapter Eight

1. Marriage record, Menard County, Menard, Texas, 18 January, 1898, book two, page 34.

2. There are numerous sources for information about this Hardin killing of Turman and most of those sources have publicized information that conflicts with the official court records. Therefore, nearly all of the facts and details involving this shooting are provided from the trial transcripts and from Gip Hardin's appeal unless otherwise listed. Those proceedings seem to provide both prosecutor and defense attorneys' arguments.

3. Communication with Ms. Linda Rudd. She wrote: My husband is a second cousin four-times removed to James Gipson "Gip" Hardin. At the time of Gip Hardin's death, he was a laborer at the International Ship Building Corporation on Hog Island, Philadelphia, Pennsylvania. I will attach a copy of his funeral record. It shows the charges for his funeral were charged to his sister, Mrs. Nannie Wyatt (Nannie Dixon Hardin), of Fort Worth, Texas, and to International Ship Building Corp. Your information about his helping to freight horses to Europe during World War I may be incorrect. The informant on his death certificate was his sister, Nannie Wyatt [*sic*, Witt].

Chapter Nine

1. Marohn, Richard C. 1995. *The Last Gunfighter: John Wesley Hardin*. College Station, TX: Creative Publishing Company. p. 320.

2. Donna Tomlinson, descendant of Mary Lucinda Bundrant Barefoot, personal interview, Mar,

2008.

3. United States Federal census records, 1860, Bastrop, TX; 1870, Gatesville, Coryell Co., TX.

4. *Ibid*, Donna Tomlinson.

5. Lipscomb County marriage records database 1887-1900.

6. Doug Hitchcock, great grandson of Ida Mae Croussore, 2008; LDS Church Ancestral File.

7. Larry J. Woods, "Gunfighters and Lawmen," *Wild West Magazine*, Feb. , 2006; Hardin Family history, M. Hardin.

8. Hitchcock, Doug, personal interview, Jan, 2010.

9. Metz, Leon, 1996, *John Wesley Hardin: Dark Angel of Texas*, Mangan Books, El Paso, Texas, p. 211.

10. *Historic San Marcos: "An Overview of Its Selected Texas Historic Landmarks"* Aug, 2009. Tallmadge and Hudson then operated a hardware store in San Marcos. An artesian well was finished in 1896.

11. Marriage record, Kimble Co. Courthouse, TX.

12. Texas Land records, 1901.

13. Newspaper article-*Colorado Clipper*, Wednesday, May 8, 1901

14. No record remains in the Scurry County District Clerk's files. Information obtained from personal interview with Don M. Jay, direct descendant of the Hardin clan.

15. Ibid; *Colorado Clipper*.

16. *Dallas Morning News*, 5-29-1901.

17. Morris Hardin, note found at Jeff Hardin's gravesite.

Chapter Ten

1. Taped interview with Charles Snowden, half-brother to John L. Snowden, undated but circa 1950s.

2. *Ibid*

3. Larry J. Woods, "Gunfighters and Lawmen", *Wild West Magazine*, Feb. , 2006; Hardin Family history, M. Hardin

4. From a biography written by an unnamed descendant who wrote: "Jeff was in Bastrop, Texas, trading saddles when a deal went bad, and Jeff was shot in a gunfight in the top part of the right lung. He rode without medical attention to Austin, where a friend took him to Junction by wagon to his brother Gip's place, where he rested and was returned to good health."

5. Taped interview Charles Snowden.

6. *Ibid.*

7. Newspaper article-*Colorado Clipper*, May 8, 1901.

8. Charles Snowden.

9. *Ibid.*

10. *Ibid.*

11. Interview with Jeff D. Hardin, grandson of Jeff and Mary Taylor Hardin. December, 2012.

Chapter Eleven

1. Cherokee is an unincorporated community in San Saba County in western Central Texas. According to the *Handbook of Texas*, the community had an estimated population of 175 in 2000.

2. According to the *Handbook of Texas*, the community of Cherokee, Texas, had an estimated population of 175 in 2000.

3. In 1887, J. M. Stephens, the local railway agent, renamed Bennett Station to Detroit for his former home in Michigan. Because of its location on the railroad the town soon became an im-

portant trading center and shipping point for area farmers.

4. Metz, Leon, *John Wesley Hardin, Dark Angel of Texas*, Norman, OK, University of Oklahoma Press, 1996; 141-143.

5. *Ibid*, 135, 136

Chapter Twelve

1. Pritchett, Jewell G. and Black, Erma Barfoot, *Kent County and Its People*, self-published, 1983.

2. Jay, Don, conversation in 2012.

3. Hardin, Jeff D., grandson of Jeff D. Hardin. Communication and copy of Hardin's stable ledger.

4. Federal U.S. Census record of Johnson County, Texas, 1880.

Chapter Thirteen

1. Hardin, Cleve, unpublished and undated journal.

2. Marker Title: Site of Creed Taylor Ranch Home - City: Junction - Year Marker Erected: 1967 — Marker Location: 19 miles East of Junction Via FM 479 on private road just west of James River about 1/2 mile off FM 479 (private property.) Marker Text: A two-story ranch house of native stone was built here in 1869-71 by Creed Taylor, veteran of war of 1846. Considered the finest home west of San Antonio, it burned in 1926. Rebuilt by Dillard Stapp, it again burned down in 1956. Taylor (1819-1906) fought in the Battle of Gonzales in 1835, and later in the Battle of Concepcion and the Siege of Bexar. Joined the Texas Rangers in 1840 and fought in Plum Creek Battle. In 1841, he joined Rangers, serving under Capt. Jack Hays in Bandera Pass Indian fight, Battle of Salado, and the Mexican War of 1846.

3. Hardin, Cleve, *journal*.

4. *Ibid*.

5. Wilkerson, Lynn, interview, August, 2011. She relayed stories told by an aunt about the Waddles. According to Leta Waddle Horine, granddaughter of Leta Minnie Taylor married Joseph Lee Moses Waddle and her sister, Lennelle (Nell) married a Mr. Joy. Mary Taylor married Jeff Hardin, brother of John Wesley Hardin. After Jeff Hardin was killed, Mary married Mr. Blount and they later divorced. Mary had three Hardin sons, Buster, Joe, and Cleve, and with Mr. Blount, two daughters, Jetty and Bertha. Taylor daughters, Nell, Mary, and Leta Minnie migrated from Texas to Arizona with their spouses and children in covered wagons. Nell Joy and family settled around Globe, Arizona. Mary Hardin Blount and sons settled west of Phoenix around Tolleson/Buckeye. Lettie Minnie Taylor Waddle and family settled in Casa Grande, AZ. Lettie Waddle told descendants that it was Mr. Joy that got the information out of her father, Creed Taylor, that was used for the book based on Creed Taylor's life, *Tall Men with Long Rifles* by James T. DeShields. [Published by Naylor, 1935 and rare.] She and sister Mary resented the fact that they never even got a copy of the book based on their father's narration. The family was skeptical about the credibility of the stories supposedly related by Creed Taylor and passed into the Texas History literature by DeShields and believed the author embezzled the truth concerning their father and questioned the credibility of many details throughout the book. The only problem with these reminiscences is that there is no evidence that DeShields ever talked to Taylor and there is ample circumstantial evidence that Taylor and DeShields never communicated or even met. According to research by Charlie Yates, In Search of Creed Taylor, a man named John Warren Hunter 1846-1915, sold his unpublished manuscript to DeShields in which Hunter had interviewed Creed Taylor numerous times and re-cording his exploits. If true, Mr. Joy would not have been the one to provide interview records to author DeShields.

6. Hardin, Cleve, *journal*. Cleve's uncle Joe Waddle married Leta Minnie Taylor, sister of Cleve's mother Mary. The Wddle family had moved to Peck Mining District, Yavapai, Arizona before 1910 and returned prior to 1917. It is likely they talked the Blounts into making the move.

7. *Ibid*.

8. *Ibid*.

9. *Ibid.*

10. *Ibid.*

11. *Ibid*

12. Jay, Don, Interview August, 2010 and Hardin, Morse, interview December, 2011.

Chapter Fifteen

1. The Epperson-Brown-Jonischkies Cemetery, is located "One mile south of the Rabke Church... on Stehele Lane [. . .] on private property[;] to the left of this lane about two hundred yards back in the weeds." Patsy Goebel and Karen Gohmert. *Cemetery Records of DeWitt County, Texas,* Vol. III, 54. The inventory lists thirty-three marked graves. Only three are Browns: R.H., November 23, 1851-November 18, 1875; Miriam, October 9, 1816-March 28, 1878; and T. Josephine, August 10, 1841-November 26, 1862. Sarah Ann Epperson, the wife of Samuel Epperson, is shown as "nee Brown." H.B. Boston, who prepared the 1873 treaty of peace, is also buried here (October 12, 1817-July 26, 1875).

2. Although perhaps a misunderstanding of the father's name, enumerator A.W. Hicks did write "Palestearn", a misspelling of the word, "palestrian", meaning of or pertaining to the palestrea, a reference to a large arena for physical athletic activities.

3. DeWitt County federal census, enumerated October 4, 1850 by A.W. Hicks, 126A. Here Mr. Brown claimed $200 worth of real estate, and was a native of Tennessee, as were his wife and first three children. Joseph Brown was the first child born in Texas.

4. DeWitt County federal census, enumerated June 8, 1860 by John R. Foster, 458B.

5. Of special interest to some WWHA members, household number 40, only a few doors preceding that of the Browns and Eppersons, was the residence of Wyatt Hanks. One of the Hanks children grew up to be a member of the Cassidy-Longabaugh gang. Orlando Camillo Hanks gained fame in his adulthood in his own way. After participating in the successful robbery of a Great Northern train near Wagner, Montana, he returned to Texas where, on April 16, 1902, he was shot and killed resisting arrest by lawmen in San Antonio. See Dan L. Thrapp. *Encyclopedia of Frontier Biography*, Vol. III, G-O, 612-13. Spokane: The Arthur H. Clark Company, 1990. He was buried in a San Antonio Cemetery but his grave is not marked.

6. The R. H. Brown headstone was literally unburied, exhumed as it were, as through the years It had sunk beneath the surface in the soft ground of the cemetery. The location of the Brown family plot was known, a space approximately 18 x 8 feet. When visited the first time by this writer in 1990 considerable time was spent cutting and removing weeds to search the ground itself. With probes and small shovels and bare hands the buried stone was unearthed. The stone, when cleaned, revealed the names, birth and death dates of three members of the Brown family: Miriam, T. Josephine and Reuben H. The "Brown Gravestone Recovery Party" consisted of Marjorie Burnett Hyatt, Robert S. Giles, Patsy Goebel, Robert Alman and Chuck Parsons. See the *Newsletter of the National Outlaw and Lawman History Association* (NOLA), Vol. XV, No. 4, June 1, 1990, 3.

7. Victor M. Rose. *The Texas Vendetta; or, The Sutton-Taylor Feud*, 52. New York: J. J. Little and Co., 1880. Facsimile edition by Ed Bartholomew, The Frontier Book Company of Houston, 1956.

8. The peace treaty appears in full in Robert C. Sutton's history, *The Sutton-Taylor Feud*, 48. Quanah, Tex., Nortex Press, 1974.

9. John J. "Jack" Helm was elected sheriff of DeWitt County on December 3, 1869; then appointed by General J.J. Reynolds on March 23, 1870, and served until his death in 1873 at the hands of Hardin and Jim Taylor. He was followed in office by William J. Weisiger, appointed on October 11, 1873, elected December 2, 1873 and reelected three times, serving until November 16, 1881. Sammy Tise. *Texas County Sheriffs*,157. Hallettsville, Tex., Privately printed, 1989.

10. The killing of Wiley Washington Pridgen is discussed in Parsons, *The Sutton-Taylor Feud: The Deadliest Blood Feud in Texas*, 144-45. Denton: The University of North Texas Press, 2009.

11. *Cuero Weekly Star*, January 23, 1874.

12. The DeWitt County federal census, enumerated by Willis Fawcett, shows Armstead Johnson, a black stock hand working for Charles W. Moore, a stock raiser. Johnson was then twenty-one years of age; his wife was Sarah, listed as a domestic servant, and they had one son, "Simps", seven years of age, all born in Texas, 233A.

13. The Gonzales County federal census, enumerated by M.H. Beaty, shows the Archibald McVea Sr. family, widower, with sons William, thirty-three; James [Gladney, or Gladden], twenty-seven; and Archibald Jr., twenty-two, 450B. Enumerated August 23, 1870. Their post office was Belmont.

14. The DeWitt County federal census, enumerated by Willis Fawcett, shows John Kron as a forty-nine year old merchant, born in Prussia. He is living in the household of F.W. Kron, perhaps a younger brother, thirty-four years of age, listed as a "Merchant's Clerk." In the same household is C.B., thirty-one, and Anna, twenty-eight. The Krons also had two domestic servants working for them. John Kron claimed $4500 worth of real estate and $20,000 of personal estate. He also was a successful merchant.

15. *Cuero Weekly Star*, January 23, 1874.

16. *Cuero Weekly Star*, April 8, 1874.

17. *Ibid.*, June 11, 1874.

18. Robert C. Sutton, *op. cit.*, 14.

19. Capt. L.H. McNelly's report to Adj. Gen. William Steele, August 31, 1874. Original in the Texas State Library and Archives, Austin.

20. As yet little is known of Sheriff Fred L. Busch. The Calhoun County federal census, enumerated by Henry W. Coustalte, shows he was then thirty-three years of age and a native of Germany, occupation sheriff. His wife, Martha C., age twenty-seven, was also a native of Germany. The three children were all born in Texas, 302B.

21. For Taylor's escape see Parsons, *The Sutton-Taylor Feud*, 205-06.

22. *Galveston Daily News*, November 19, 1875.

23. *Galveston Weekly News*, November 22, 1875.

24. *Galveston Daily News*, November 23, 1875.

25. *Austin Daily Democratic Statesman*, January 6, 1876. See also Parsons' "Bill Sutton Avenged: The Death of Jim Taylor" in the NOLA *Quarterly*, Vol. 3, March 1973, 3-5.

26. Originally, the graves of Arnold and Hendricks were marked only with wooden boards. They were replaced with granite stones in July 1988. A special program was organized by Marjorie Burnett Hyatt with some seventy people in attendance, including numerous descendants of both sides of the feud. The granite headstones were donated by Joe and Carol Solansky Marble & Granite Works of Gonzales. A.R. Hendricks remains a mysterious figure of the feud, not even what his initials stood for is known. He had served with Captain McNelly from July 25, 1874 to February 24, 1875, with the rank of sergeant.

Chapter Sixteen
1. Tennille's four marriages were: to Brown on July 2, 1846; to a Miss Kelso on July 19, 1853; to Ann J. Sample and then to Amanda Jane Billings on July 7, 1855. *Tom Tennille and the Disappearance of Jim Clements: Echoes of the Sutton-Taylor Feud and Texas Reconstruction* by Wayne Tennille, p. 41

2. Victor M. Rose. *The Texas Vendetta; or, the Sutton-Taylor Feud*. New York: J. J. Little & Co., 1880; facsimile edition by Ed Bartholomew, The Frontier Press, Houston, Texas, 1956.

3. For a treatment of Hardin's problems with the Texas State police see this author's essay "The War on the Texas State Police: John Wesley Hardin and his Conflicts with Authority" in *Central Texas Studies: Journal of the Central Texas Historical Association*, Vol. 2, 2017, pp. 24-39. The unique full-length treatment of the Texas State Police remains *The Governor's Hounds: The Texas State Police, 1870-1873* by Barry A. Crouch and Donaly E. Brice, published by University of Texas

Press, 2011.

4. Some writers have identified Jim Taylor and Hardin as cousins, but this is an error. Hardin was not related to the Taylors. Part of the confusion may be due to the fact that Hardin's younger brother, Jefferson Davis Hardin, married Mary Taylor, a daughter of Creed Taylor, but that was years after the feud had ended and after the death of John Wesley Hardin.

5. This is in error. The killing of Cox and Christman happened on July 15; three days later on the eighteenth, Hardin and Taylor killed Jack Helm at Albuquerque in Gonzales County.

6. The published writings of "Pidge," actually T.C. Robinson, a McNelly ranger, have been gathered and published in book form by Parsons, in *"Pidge," Texas Ranger*, published by Texas A&M University Press, 2013.

Chapter Nineteen

1. Family tradition refers to letters of Mrs. Tom Duderstadt and her daughter, Mrs. A.L. Vaughn. Bockius was related only in that he married the widow of George C. Tennille, whose daughter had married into the Duderstadt family.

2. These Texas Military Records are presently in the Texas State Archives, Austin, Texas.

3. Confederate War Records available through the General Services Administration, National Archives, Washington, D.C.

4. Duderstadt, Earnest F. *Duderstadt Family History*, privately printed, March 1963, Ingram, Texas, 21.

5. *Duderstadt Family History*, 20-21.

6. Hardin, John Wesley. *The Life of John Wesley Hardin, as Written by Himself*. Smith & Moore, Seguin, Texas, 1896, 88. Reprinted by the University of Oklahoma Press, 1961, 1966. Page references are to the Oklahoma reprint.

7. *Austin Daily Democratic Statesman*, June 11, 1874, reprinted article from *The Comanche Chief*. Waldron may be a misspelling of the name *Waldrip* as other Hardin associates were named Waldrip.

8. Affidavit of John Wesley Hardin, January 1, 1894, 3. Presently among the Hardin papers, Texas State Library.

9. *Austin Daily Democratic Statesman*, June 17, 1874, reprinted from *The Denison News*.

10. Green, Major William M. "Breaking Up the Lawless Element in Texas" in *Frontier Times*, May, 1924, Vol.1, #8, 4-5.

11. Hardin, *The Life*, 101.

12. Green, 5.

13. Hardin, 107-08.

14. *San Antonio Daily Herald*, June 30, 1874. Reprinted article from *The Cuero Star*.

15. Details of the escape from the lynch mob and Joe Sunday are among correspondence of Mrs. Tom Duderstadt, principal letters being those of March 30, 1972 and April 2, 1976.

16. Details of Bockius's later life are from Mrs. Tom Duderstadt's correspondence.

17. Nordyke, Lewis. *John Wesley Hardin Texas Gunman*. William Morrow & Company, New York, 1957, 253-54. Nordyke, without identifying sources, wrote: "[T]he presiding judge at Sedan was two miles out of Gonzales with the all-important returns. This presiding judge was Doc Bockius, the mysterious little man who had once quit his store at Sedan to work as a Wes Hardin cowboy and barely escaped with his life." One obvious error here, of course, is that the "store at Sedan" did not come into existence until after 1874 with Tennille's death, which was after Bockius's escape from the lynch mob.

Chapter Twenty

1. Genealogical information on children of William Riley and Elizabeth Taylor from *Taylor Fam-*

ily History: Descendants of Josiah Taylor and Hephzibeth Luker, 25. Marjorie Lee Burnett, compiler. Smiley, Tex., Sandies Creek Press, 2003.

2. Chuck Parsons. *The Sutton-Taylor Feud: The Deadliest Blood Feud in Texas*, 52-56. Denton: University of North Texas Press, 2009.

3. DeWitt County, Texas Federal Census, enumerated July --, 1860 by John R. Foster, 476A-476B.

4. For details on John and Phillip Taylor's killing of the two military men in Fort Mason see Parsons, op. cit., 28-29.

5. DeWitt County, Texas Federal Census, enumerated July --, 1870 by Willis Fawcett, 244A.

6. The shooting of Pitkin Taylor and his funeral see Jack Hays Day, *The Sutton Taylor Feud*, 116-20. San Antonio, Tex., Sid Murray & Sons, Printers, 1937; and Parsons, op. cit., 116-20.

7. Day, op. cit., 23; Parsons, op. cit., 150-54.

8. Fred L. Busch was elected Calhoun County sheriff December 2, 1873; re-elected February 15, 1876, November 5, 1878 and served until November 2, 1880. Sammy Tise. *Texas County Sheriffs*, 81. Hallettsville, Tex. Privately printed, 1989.

9. Parsons, op. cit., 205-06.

10. Killing of Reuben H. Brown is reported in the *Galveston Weekly News*, November 22, 1875 as well as the *New York Times*, November 19, 1875 and also see Parsons, op. cit., 206-07.

11. For the death of Jim Taylor, Arnold and Hendricks, see Parsons, op. cit., 208-11.

12. *Victoria Advocate*, July 13, 1878.

13. Arrest of Taylor by Lieutenant Foster, see telegram from Coleman County Clerk L.C. Williamson to Adjutant General William Steele, April 15, 1877. Original in Adjutant General Files, Texas State Archives.

14. *Victoria Advocate*, July 13, 1878.

15. *Victoria Advocate*, January 17, 1880.

16. DeWitt County Federal Census, enumerated June 17, 1880 by R.M. Forbes [?], 368B. In this enumeration we learn the jailer is Louis Demoss, the man who replaced Reuben H. Brown as City Marshal of Cuero.

17. Affidavit recorded in the Kimble County, Texas courthouse, Junction, Texas. Photocopy provided by Frederica Wyatt of Junction. The two affiants were William Walter Taylor, a son of William P. "Buck" Taylor, killed during the feud; Thomas Jefferson Bailey married Elizabeth Taylor Jr., daughter of William Riley and Elizabeth Tumlinson Taylor on May 11, 1865 in DeWitt County. Notary public Coke Stevenson later became governor of Texas, serving from 1941-1947.

Author Biographies

Norman Wayne Brown is a retired Air Force disabled veteran and a retired Texas State Parole Officer. He writes about the Wild West with seven books and dozens of magazine articles. His latest book, *Man Hunter in Indian County, Deputy US Marshal George Redman Tucker*, Eakin Press, has received five-star reviews.

Chuck Parsons, a Texan by choice, was raised in Iowa and Minnesota. Texas history has always held a fascination for him, and he has authored several books about the state's best-known characters from history. His writings include *The Sutton-Taylor Feud*; *Jack Helm: A Victim of Texas Reconstruction Violence*; *King Fisher: The Short Life and Elusive Legend of a Texas Desperado*; *Captain John R. Hughes: Lone Star Ranger*; *Texas Ranger Lee Hall: From the Red River to the Rio Grande* among others.

www.ingramcontent.com/pod-product-compliance
Lightning Source LLC
Chambersburg PA
CBHW070034100426
42740CB00013B/2690